Praise for C
The Myth of a Po

*Reading this book makes you look at our nation with new eyes.
The simplistic notion that Americans are more polarized than
ever before is brilliantly and persuasively put to rest. We're not
more polarized; our choices are. That's a message everyone concerned about civic life should absorb.*

—Jane Eisner, *The Philadelphia Inquirer;*
Senior fellow, University of Pennsylvania

*This book tells the truth about America: the culture war is a
myth. Americans are largely united across a wide range of attitudes, values, and beliefs—even abortion and homosexuality.
Clear, well written, and packed with evidence presented in an
easy-to-digest format, this book is a must-read for anyone who
wants to rip away the veil of illusion and propaganda to get to
the facts.*

—Wayne Baker, Professor of Sociology and Professor of
Management & Organizations, University of Michigan;
author, *America's Crisis of Values: Reality and Perception*

*For anyone who still thinks that ordinary Americans are hope-
lessly polarized,* Culture Wars? *documents with overwhelming
evidence that they are not.*

—Alan Wolfe, Professor of Political Science and Director of
the Boisi Center for Religion and American Public Life at
Boston College; author, *One Nation, After All*

". . . Culture War? The Myth of a Polarized America *makes a
compelling case that pundits and journalists have it all wrong.*"

From MSNBC.com, Jan. 19, 2005 (by Alex Johnson)

Culture War?

The Myth of a Polarized America

MORRIS P. FIORINA
STANFORD UNIVERSITY

WITH

SAMUEL J. ABRAMS
HARVARD UNIVERSITY

AND

JEREMY C. POPE
BRIGHAM YOUNG UNIVERSITY

New York • Boston • San Francisco
London • Toronto • Sydney • Tokyo • Singapore • Madrid
Mexico City • Munich • Paris • Cape Town • Hong Kong • Montreal

Executive Editor:	Eric Stano
Senior Marketing Manager:	Elizabeth Fogarty
Production Manager:	Stacey Kulig
Project Coordination, Text Design, and Electronic Page Makeup:	Thompson Steele Production Services, Inc.
Senior Cover Design Manager:	Nancy Danahy
Cover Designer:	Base Art Co.
Cover Illustration:	Getty Images
Manufacturing Manager:	Mary Fischer
Printer and Binder:	R. R. Donnelley & Sons Company
Cover Printer:	Phoenix Color Corporation

Library of Congress Cataloging-in-Publication Data

Fiorina, Morris P.
    Culture war? : the myth of a polarized America / Morris P. Fiorina ; with
Samuel J. Abrams, and Jeremy C. Pope. -- 2nd ed.
        p. cm.
    Includes bibliographical references and index.
    ISBN 0-321-36606-9 (pbk. : alk. paper)
    1. Culture conflict--United States. 2. Politics and culture--United
States. 3. United States--Politics and government--2001- I. Abrams,
Samuel J., 1980- II. Pope, Jeremy, 1973- III. Title.
    HN59.2.F564 2005b
    306.20973--dc22   2005027620

Please visit us at www.ablongman.com

ISBN 0-321-36606-9
ISBN 0-321-40899-3

1 2 3 4 5 6 7 8 9 10—DOH—07 06 05 04

To the tens of millions

of mainstream Americans

who have never heard

of the culture war

Contents

✣

Preface to the Second Edition

When we arrived at our offices on the morning after the 2004 elections, the message lights on our phones were blinking and our e-mail inboxes were overflowing. During the few months that intervened between the July publication of the first edition of this book and the November election, we had spoken with numerous print and broadcast journalists, many of whom took seriously the message of the first edition—that America was not a deeply divided country. Rather, we were a nation whose people shared a great deal of common ground, a condition obscured by the self-indulgent battling of a fractious political class.

But, many of the messages that morning said, the 2004 voting was highly polarized, and voters' concern with "moral values" had reelected President Bush. Did this not indicate that our argument had been wrong, or at least that it was no longer right? Within a few hours it became clear that the prevailing story line about moral values was almost completely wrong, a fact widely recognized by analysts and journalists within a few days, but too late to prevent hard-core social conservatives from staking a claim that they had reelected George Bush, and hard-core liberal Democrats from indulging in an orgy of emotional venting.[1]

In fact, data from the 2004 election season reinforce the message of the first edition. While the process of partisan "sorting" continues—for two decades liberals and conservatives increasingly have been finding their way into the "correct" parties—polarized partisan ideologues are a distinct minority of the American population. For the most part Americans continue to be ambivalent, moderate, and pragmatic, in contrast to the cocksure extremists and ideologues who dominate our public political life.

In this second edition we update our description of the political positions of the American public with newly released data from the 2004 National Election Study, the 2004 General Social Survey, the 2004 exit polls, and various other surveys. A new chapter (Chapter 2) outlines our argument which, in retrospect, was too spread out in the first edition, leading to unnecessary confusion among some readers. Another new chapter (Chapter 8) examines the 2004 election and the issues it raises for the future. The outcomes of most elections hinge on multiple issues and considerations, of course, but if we were to emphasize one or two, analysis of the 2004 voting identifies leadership and security concerns, with moral values well down the list. And if commentators

---

[1] As David Brooks wrote shortly after the election, "Every election year, we in the commentariat come up with a story line to explain the result, and the story line has to have two features. First, it has to be completely wrong. Second, it has to reassure liberals that they are morally superior to the people who just defeated them." We agree with Brooks's first assertion but we would amend the second by substituting "losers" for "liberals." Recall that after attempts to exploit the Monica Lewinsky scandal backfired on Congressional Republicans in 1998, frustrated conservatives declared that the culture war was over and they had lost—the election results showed that Americans were a bunch of amoral greedheads who only cared about the accumulations in their 401ks. It is psychologically easier for losers—liberals or conservatives—to blame wrong-headed voters rather than admit that reasonable voters rejected their principles and platforms. David Brooks, "The Values-Vote Myth," www.nytimes.com, November 6, 2004.

insist on crediting a particular group for the reelection of George Bush—a questionable exercise in a close election—that group would be women rather than religious conservatives.

We wish to thank the numerous colleagues who offered comments and suggestions at various seminars and workshops. And we also offer our sincere thanks to the many journalists who talked to us in good faith and communicated what we had written to a wider audience.[2] We hope they will continue that educational effort.

—MORRIS P. FIORINA

[2] A task they performed well beyond any of our expectations. See Wayne Baker, "Social Science in the Public Interest: To What Extent Did the Media Cover 'Culture War? The Myth of a Polarized America?,' " *The Forum*, 3 (2005), www.bepress.com/forum/vol3/iss2/art4

Preface to the
First Edition

The late Senator Daniel Patrick Moynihan used to say that we all were entitled to our own opinions, but not to our own facts. This book uses simple facts to confront a distorted political debate in this country. Increasingly, we hear politicians, interest group leaders, and assorted "activists" speak half-truths to the American people. They tell us that the United States is split right down the middle, bitterly and deeply divided about national issues, when the truth is more nearly the opposite. Americans are closely divided, but we are not deeply divided, and we are closely divided because many of us are ambivalent and uncertain, and consequently reluctant to make firm commitments to parties, politicians, or policies. We divide evenly in elections or sit them out entirely because we instinctively seek the center while the parties and candidates hang out on the extremes.

How can the prevailing view assert the direct opposite? Mainly for want of contradiction by those who know better. We should not expect political actors to speak truthfully to us. For them, words are weapons, and the standard of success is electoral and legislative victory, not education or enlightenment. We may regret that perspective, but it should not surprise us. What is more surprising, and more disappointing, is that inaccurate claims and charges made by members of the political class go uncorrected by those who have some occupational responsibility to correct them, namely, members of the media and academic communities.

Increasingly, the media have abandoned their informational role in favor of an entertainment role. If colorful claims have news value, well then, why worry about their truth value? Don't let facts get in the way of a good story line. As for those of us in academia, we roll our eyes at the television, shake our heads while reading the newspapers, and lecture our students on the fallacies reported in the media, but few of us go beyond that. Mostly we talk to and write for each other.

In the past few years there have been increasing indications (see Chapter 1) that high-level political actors are beginning to believe in the distorted picture of American politics that they have helped to paint. This development threatens to make the distorted picture a self-fulfilling prophecy as a polarized political class abandons any effort to reach out toward the great middle of the country. That threat has motivated this ivory tower academic to attempt to provide his fellow citizens with a picture of American politics that is very different from the one they see portrayed on their televisions and described in their newspapers and magazines, a picture I think they will recognize as a more accurate reflection of their social surroundings.

My thanks to the Hoover Institution and Stanford University for the financial support that made this book possible. In particular, their support enabled me to engage two able, hardworking collaborators, Samuel Abrams and Jeremy Pope, who compiled and organized data, questioned my arguments and conclusions, and clarified the presentation. Thanks also to seminar participants at Harvard University, Northwestern University, and Stanford University for their helpful comments and suggestions about the analyses reported in these pages. Joshua Dunn, The College of William & Mary; Clyde Wilcox, Georgetown University; Jack Citrin, University of California, Berkeley; Kent Jennings, University of California, Santa Barbara; and David Edwards, University of Texas reviewed the manuscript and provided useful comments. Sam Popkin offered valuable suggestions for making the argument clearer, and as always, Bonnie Honig urged me to give more thought to broader issues.

—MORRIS P. FIORINA

A member of that tiny elite that comments publicly about political currents (probably some fraction of 1 percent of a population) spends most of his time in informal communication about politics with others in the same select group. He rarely encounters a conversation in which his assumptions of shared contextual grasp of political ideas are challenged. . . . It is largely from his informal communications that he learns how "public opinion" is changing and what the change signifies, and he generalizes facilely from these observations to the bulk of the broader public.

Philip Converse, "The Nature of Belief Systems in Mass Publics," in *Ideology and Discontent*, ed. David Apter (New York: Free Press, 1964): 206–261

CHAPTER I

Culture War?

*There is a religious war going on in this country, a cultural
war as critical to the kind of nation we shall be as the Cold
War itself, for this war is for the soul of America.*[1]

With those ringing words insurgent candidate Pat Buchanan
fired up his supporters at the 1992 Republican National Convention. To be sure, not all the assembled delegates cheered
Buchanan's call to arms, which was at odds with the "kinder, gen-
tler" image that incumbent President George H. W. Bush had
attempted to project. Indeed, Republican professionals expressed
concern about the "family values" emphasis of the convention in
general, and Buchanan's remarks in particular.[2] Their concerns

---

[1] This quotation appears in slightly different forms throughout the literature, probably because it was
written up differently by journalists who covered the speech and/or read slightly different versions of it.
This version is quoted in Nancy Davis and Robert Robinson, "A War for America's Soul?" In Rhys
Williams, ed., *Cultural Wars in American Politics* (New York: Aldine de Gruyter, 1997): 39.
[2] Andrew Rosenthal, "The 1992 Campaign: Issues—'Family Values,'" *New York Times*, September 21,
1992: 1.

proved well founded: elections analysts later included negative reaction to the convention and Buchanan's fiery words among the factors contributing to the defeat of President Bush, albeit factors of lesser importance than the struggling economy and repudiation of his "Read my lips, no new taxes" pledge.[3]

Political campaigns encourage fiery rhetoric, of course, most of which dies down after the campaign. So, too, did talk of a culture war wax and wane during the mid-1990s. Buchanan seemed vindicated in 1994 when the Republicans captured Congress in the "year of the angry white male." The story line held that white men under economic pressure were livid about gays, guns, immigration, affirmative action, and Hillary, and turned in frustration to the Gingrich Republicans. But in 1996 talk of a culture war waned as hapless Republican presidential candidate Robert Dole demanded of a satisfied country "where's the outrage?" Then in 1998 discussion of the culture war erupted anew, fueled by the Monica Lewinsky scandal. And except for a brief period in the aftermath of 9/11 the flames have not diminished since.

The "culture war" refers to a displacement of the classic economic conflicts that animated twentieth-century politics in the advanced democracies by newly emergent moral and religious ones. The literature generally attributes Buchanan's inspiration to a 1991 book, *Culture Wars*, by sociologist James Davison Hunter, who divided Americans into the culturally "orthodox" and the culturally "progressive" and argued that increasing conflict was

---

3 Paul Abramson, John Aldrich, and David Rohde, *Change and Continuity in the 1992 Elections.* (Washington, DC: CQ Press, 1994): 43–44, 137. For a detailed analysis of the association between family values issues and the 1992 voting see Laura Arnold and Herbert Weisberg, "Parenthood, Family Values, and the 1992 Presidential Election." *American Politics Quarterly* 24 (1996): 194–220.

inevitable.[4] In a later book provocatively titled *Before the Shooting Begins*, Hunter writes,

> *. . . when cultural impulses this momentous vie against each other to dominate public life, tension, conflict, and perhaps even violence are inevitable.*[5]

Not surprisingly, no one has embraced the idea of the culture war more enthusiastically than the journalistic community, ever alert for subjects that have "news value." Conflict, of course, is high in news value. Disagreement, division, polarization, battles, and war make better copy than agreement, consensus, moderation, cooperation, and peace. Thus, the culture war frame fits the news values of journalists who cover American politics. Their reports tell us that contemporary voters are deeply divided on moral issues:

> *. . . the real emotional splits in the country lie in gut-level social issues: They are the topics that move Americans in their everyday lives, and the ones that actually draw the lines separating the two parties today.*[6]

> *The divide went deeper than politics. It reached into the nation's psyche . . . It was the moral dimension that kept Bush in the race.*[7]

---

[4] *Culture Wars: The Struggle to Define America* (New York: Basic Books, 1991).
[5] *Before the Shooting Begins: Searching for Democracy in America's Culture War* (New York Free Press. 1995): xx.
[6] John Harwood and Shailagh Murray, "Split Society: Year After Year, The Big Divide In Politics Is Race," *Wall Street Journal*, December 19, 2002: A1.
[7] David Broder, "One Nation, Divisible; Despite Peace, Prosperity, Voters Agree to Disagree," *Washington Post*, November 8, 2000: A1.

And close elections do not reflect indifferent, uncertain, or ambivalent voters; rather, close elections reflect a standoff between two large blocs of deeply committed partisans:

> *When George W. Bush took office, half the country cheered and the other half seethed.*[8]

> *Such political divisions cannot easily be shifted by any president, let alone in two years, because they reflect deep demographic divisions . . . . The 50-50 nation appears to be made up of two big, separate voting blocks, with only a small number of swing voters in the middle.*[9]

The 2000 election brought pictorial representation of the culture war in the form of the red and blue map of the United States (the 2004 version is reproduced on the inside front cover of this book). Vast areas of the southern and midwestern heartland emerged from the election as Republican red. But the huge expanses of red territory contained relatively few people per square mile. The much smaller areas of Democratic blue contained the more populous cosmopolitan states of the east and west coasts and the Great Lakes. Often commentators accompanied such colorful maps with polling factoids intended to illustrate the cultural divide: the probability that a white, gun-toting, born-again, rural southern male voted for Al Gore was about as tiny as the probability that a feminist, agnostic, professional, urban northern female voted for George W. Bush, although few asked how many Americans fell into such tightly bounded categories.

---

[8] Jill Lawrence, "Behind Its United Front, Nation Divided As Ever," *USA Today*, February 18, 2002: A1.
[9] "On His High Horse," *The Economist*, November 9, 2002: 25.

For the most part pundits reified the different colors on the map, treating them as *prima facie* evidence of deep cultural divisions:

Bush knew that the landslide he had wished for in 2000 . . . had vanished into the values chasm separating the blue states from the red ones.[10]

You see the state where James Byrd was lynch-dragged behind a pickup truck until his body came apart—it's red. You see the state where Matthew Shepard was crucified on a split-rail fence for the crime of being gay—it's red. You see the state where right-wing extremists blew up a federal office building and murdered scores of federal employees—it's red. The state where an Army private who was thought to be gay was bludgeoned to death with a baseball bat, and the state where neo-Nazi skinheads murdered two African Americans because of their skin color, and the state where Bob Jones University spews its anti-Catholic bigotry: they're all red too.[11]

Claims of deep national division were standard after the 2000 elections, and few commentators challenged them.[12] On the contrary, the belief in a fractured nation continued to be expressed even by high-level political operatives:

We have two massive colliding forces. One is rural, Christian, religiously conservative. [The other] is socially tolerant, pro-choice, secular, living in New England and the Pacific coast.[13]

[10] John Kenneth White, *The Values Divide* (New Jersey: Chatham House, 2003): 171.

[11] Clinton advisor Paul Begala, as quoted in Bob Clark, "As You Were Saying . . . It's Time for Gore's Pit Bull to Practice What He Preaches," *Boston Herald*, November 18, 2000: 16.

[12] For a notable exception see Robert Samuelson, "Polarization Myths," *Washington Post*, December 3, 2003: A29.

[13] Republican pollster Bill McInturff, as quoted in "One Nation, Fairly Divisible, Under God," *The Economist*, January 20, 2001: 22.

You've got 80 percent to 90 percent of the country that look at each other like they are on separate planets.[14]

A November 2003 report of the Pew Research Center for the People & the Press led a prominent journalist to comment:

> *The red states get redder, the blue states get bluer, and the political map of the United States takes on the coloration of the Civil War.*[15]

While Andrew Kohut, director of the Pew Center, reportedly commented that

> *. . . the anger level is so high that if the demonstrators of 1968 had felt like this there would have been gunfire in the streets.*[16]

Political commentators saw a continuation, if not an intensification of the culture war as the 2004 election approached.

> *The culture war between the Red and Blue Nations has erupted again—big time—and will last until Election Day next year. Front lines are all over, from the Senate to the Pentagon to Florida to the Virginia suburbs where, at the Bush-Cheney '04 headquarters, they are blunt about the shape of the battle: "The country's split 50-50 again," a top aide told me, "just as it was in 2000."*[17]

---

[14] Matthew Dowd, Bush reelection strategist. Dowd was explaining why Bush had not tried to expand his electoral base. Quoted in Ron Brownstein, "Bush Falls to Pre-9/11 Approval Rating," *Los Angeles Times*, October 3, 2003: A1.

[15] E. J. Dionne Jr., "One Nation Deeply Divided," *Washington Post*, November 7, 2003: A31.

[16] Quoted in John Leo, "Splitting Society, Not Hairs," *US News and World Report Science & Society*, December 15, 2003: 66. Kohut may be too young to remember, but there *was* sporadic gunfire in the streets and on college campuses during the 1960s "time of troubles." We have more to say about the Pew Report in chapter 4.

[17] Howard Fineman, "Election Boils Down to a Culture War: Abortion Issue is First Skirmish in the Battle for White House." *Newsweek*, October 22, 2003: http://msnbc.msn.com/id/3225677, accessed December 12, 2003.

After the 2004 elections much of the commentary continued in this vein. Instant post-election analysis attributed President Bush's reelection to the higher turnout and increased support of Evangelical Christians (wrongly as it turned out). In response, bitterly disappointed Democratic commentators slammed the denizens of red states, whose votes reflected "fundamentalist zeal, a rage at secularity, religious intolerance, fear of and hatred for modernity"—attitudes more common "in the Muslim world, in Al Qaeda, in Saddam Hussein's Sunni loyalists" than in other democracies.[18] And,

> *Listen to what the red state citizens say about themselves, the songs they write, and the sermons they flock to. They know who they are—they are full of original sin and they have a taste for violence. The blue state citizens make the Rousseauvian mistake of thinking humans are essentially good, and so they never realize when they are about to be slugged from behind.*[19]

Even mainstream media commentators saw a "national fissure" that "remains deep and wide," and "Two Nations Under God."[20]

In sum, many contemporary observers of American politics believe that old disagreements about economics now pale in comparison to new divisions based on sexuality, morality, and religion, divisions so deep as to justify fears of violence and talk of war in describing them.[21]

---

[18] Gary Wills, "The Day the Enlightenment Went out," *New York Times*, November 4, 2004, nytimes.com.
[19] Jane Smiley, "The unteachable ignorance of the red states," slate.msn.com/id/2109218/
[20] Ronald Brownstein, "The National Fissure Remains Deep and Wide," www.latimes.com, November 3, 2004. Thomas Friedman, "Two Nations Under God," *New York Times*, November 4, 2004, nytimes.com.
[21] Of course, there is nothing new about cultural conflict in the United States—it has been a common element of our politics since the beginning of the Republic. It only seems new to today's generation of political commentators because such issues were relatively muted from the late-1930s until the mid-1960s.

This short book advances a contrary thesis: the sentiments expressed in the previously quoted pronouncements of scholars, journalists, and politicos range from simple exaggeration to sheer nonsense. Such assertions both reflect and contribute to a widespread mythology about contemporary American politics. The simple truth is that there is no culture war in the United States— no battle for the soul of America rages, at least none that most Americans are aware of. Certainly, one can find a few faux-warriors who engage in noisy skirmishes. Many of the activists in the political parties and the various cause groups do, in fact, hate each other and regard themselves as combatants in a war. But their hatreds and battles are not shared by the great mass of the American people—certainly nowhere near to "80–90 percent of the country"—who are for the most part moderate in their views and tolerant in their manner.[22] Most Americans are somewhat like the unfortunate citizens of some third-world countries who try to stay out of the crossfire while left-wing guerrillas and right-wing death squads shoot at each other.

The myth of a culture war rests on misinterpretation of election returns, a lack of comprehensive examination of public opinion data, systematic and self-serving misrepresentation by issue activists, and selective coverage by an uncritical media more concerned with news value than with getting the story right. There is little evidence that Americans' ideological or policy *positions* are more polarized today than they were two or three decades ago,

---

[22] On the whole our conclusions support the earlier findings of Alan Wolfe, *One Nation, After All* (New York: Viking, 1998). Some critics have dismissed Wolfe's findings as reflecting only the views of 200 middle class suburban families. The chapters that follow report similar findings based on an examination of the views of tens of thousands of Americans questioned in national surveys.

although their *choices* often seem to be. The explanation is that the political figures Americans evaluate are more polarized. A polarized political class makes the citizenry appear polarized, but it is largely that—an appearance.

In Chapter 2 we lay out our argument in greater detail. Chapter 3 shows that the red state versus blue state contrast grossly exaggerates the actual differences among their residents. Chapter 4 shows that the United States is not polarized along other traditional cleavage lines either. What has happened is that partisans have become better sorted into the parties than in past decades. Thus, especially at their most active levels the parties are more polarized, but most commentators fail to realize that this *partisan* polarization has only a faint reflection in *popular* polarization, so the latter certainly is not a cause of the former. Chapter 5 shows that the picture of a largely centrist population holds even when we focus on abortion, a fact now beginning to be recognized although it has been apparent for decades. Chapter 6 addresses a rapidly changing subject—attitudes toward homosexual rights—that exploded on the national scene in the form of the gay marriage issue in the spring of 2004. While there is considerable division in the population about gay rights and gay marriage, the movement toward increased acceptance of gays and lesbians in the past decade has been so strong that we believe the present divisions are largely a transitional state. Chapter 7 shows that the purported replacement of economic cleavages in the electorate by religious ones is a premature conclusion. Chapter 8 discusses the 2004 election, noting that the initial interpretation of the election as hinging on moral values was almost totally wrong. In fact, the election hinged far more on evaluations of George W. Bush's leadership, especially on security issues. Chapter 9 shows how the polarization of partisan elites can give the *appearance* that voters are shifting emphasis from economics to religion and morality, even while voter preferences stay completely stable. Finally, Chapter 10 discusses how extreme voices have come to dominate American political discourse, and how their influence might be lessened and the vast middle ground empowered.

CHAPTER 2

If America Is Not Polarized, Why Do So Many Americans Think It Is?

We worship an awesome God in the blue states, and we don't like federal agents poking around our libraries in the red states. We coach little league in the blue states and, yes, we've got some gay friends in the red states.[1]

Barack Obama's speech to the Democratic National Convention was widely applauded, in part, we suspect, because many heard it as a welcome call for reconciliation—a plea for Americans to overcome their differences and discover their commonalities. As we will show in Chapters 3–6, however, contemporary Americans are not particularly polarized in their political positions, nor

---

[1] Barack Obama, Keynote Speech to the 2004 Democratic National Convention.

have they become appreciably more so in recent decades. Widespread beliefs to the contrary notwithstanding, the notion of a deeply divided population is largely a myth.

Myths do not emerge out of thin air. Upon examination, it generally turns out that they have developed from facts or observations that are misinterpreted or otherwise transformed until many people believe that the myth is reality. In the case of the mostly mythical polarization of America, we believe that at least four contributing factors can be identified. This is not to say that there are no others, only to say that we regard these four as both clearly implicated and important.

CONTRIBUTING FACTOR #1.
CONFUSING CLOSELY DIVIDED
WITH DEEPLY DIVIDED

In one of the claims quoted in the preceding chapter a writer for the *Economist* refers to "the 50:50 nation." During the early 2000s this phrase began to appear in popular discussions of American politics, as did a similar phrase, "the 49 percent nation."[2] Such phraseology referred to the close national elections of the late 1990s, when the winning party's share repeatedly came in right around 49 percent of the popular vote:

- 1996 Clinton Vote   49.2%
- 1996 Republican House Vote   48.9
- 1998 Republican House Vote   48.9
- 2000 Gore Vote   48.4

---

[2] Michael Barone, "The 49% Nation," in Michael Barone, Richard Cohen, and Charles E. Cook Jr., eds., *The Almanac of American Politics* (Washington, DC: National Journal, 2002): 21–45.

- 2000 Republican House Vote   48.3
- 2002 Republican House Vote   52.9
- 2004 Republican Presidential Vote   50.7
- 2004 Republican House Vote   50.4

Recent national elections have been exceedingly and unusually close. In the 1992–1996–2000 election sequence, no presidential candidate won a majority of the popular vote, these elections constituting the longest such streak since the so-called "era of indecision" when no presidential candidate won a majority of the popular vote in the four elections between 1880 and 1892 inclusive.

The question is how to interpret this electoral competitiveness? Most commentators seem to believe that the answer is obvious: the American electorate is polarized. In the previously quoted words of the *Economist*, the recent close U.S. elections "*. . . reflect deep demographic divisions . . . The 50-50 nation appears to be made up of two big, separate voting blocks, with only a small number of swing voters in the middle.*" The top panel of Figure 2.1 depicts this claim graphically. Voters line up from left to right and the electorate is highly polarized: a large number of "progressives" on the left support the Democrats, a large number of "orthodox" on the right support the Republicans, and very few people occupy the middle ground. With a polarized electorate like this, elections will be very close, half the voters will cheer, and half the voters will seethe, as *USA Today* asserts.

But the U-shaped distribution in the top panel of the figure by no means is the only electoral configuration that will produce close elections. In particular, consider its inverse —the bell-shaped distribution in the bottom panel of Figure 2.1. In the lower figure most people hold moderate or centrist positions and relatively few

FIGURE 2.1
Two Very Different Close Election Scenarios

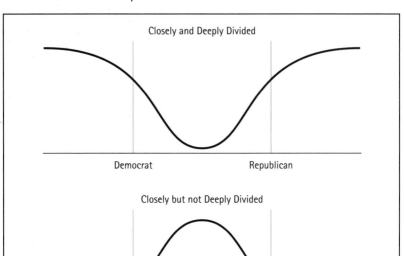

Closely and Deeply Divided

Democrat   Republican

Closely but not Deeply Divided

Democrat   Republican

are extreme ideologues. But if the Democratic and Republican parties position themselves equidistant from the center on opposite sides, then the bottom configuration, too, produces close elections. In both conditions the electorate is *closely* divided, but only in the top panel of the figure would we say that the voters are *deeply* divided. In the top panel it would be accurate to say that voters are polarized, but in the bottom panel it would be more accurate to say that most voters are ambivalent or indifferent.

When an election results in a near 50:50 outcome, the automatic interpretation seems to be that the electorate looks like the

FIGURE 2.2
Congress Has Polarized Since the 1960s

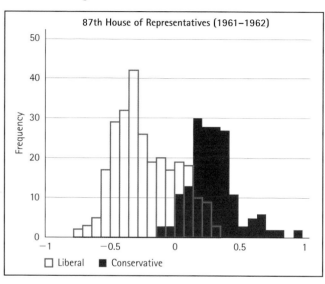

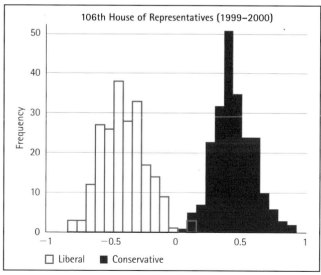

Source: Scores calculated with DW-Nominate procedure developed by Keith Poole and Howard Rosenthal. (Roll call data available online at voteview.uh.edu /default _nomdata.htm)

FIGURE 2.4
Polarization of Choices

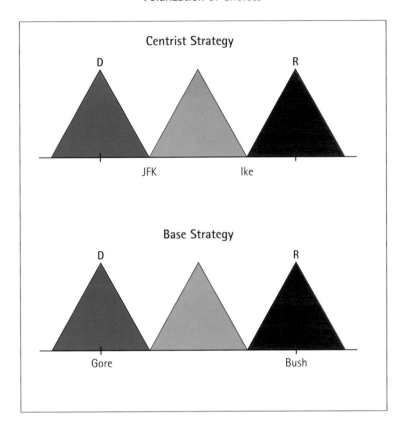

top panel of Figure 2.1. That should not be the default conclusion. Consider that when an individual voter reports that he or she is on the fence (50:50) about whom to vote for, everyone understands that there are multiple interpretations: the individual likes both candidates equally, dislikes both candidates equally, or doesn't give a damn. No one suggests that the individual is polarized. But the aggregate and individual situations are analogous. In each case a continuous variable (percent of the vote/probability of voting for a particular candidate) is compressed into a dichotomous variable (Republican or Democratic win/Republican or Democratic vote), with enormous loss of information. To illustrate, consider the map on the inside back cover of this book, which differs from the red and blue map on the front cover by coloring a state red or blue in proportion to its Republican/Democratic vote. Now most of the map is purple, reflecting the fact that most states are mixed, not totally in the camp of one party or the other. In language analogous to that used to describe individual voters, we might call such states "ambivalent" or "uncertain."

In sum, close elections may reflect equal numbers of voters who hate one candidate and love the other, voters who like or dislike both, voters who don't care much at all about either candidate, or various combinations of these conditions. *By themselves close election outcomes cannot tell us whether half the electorate hates the other half or whether everyone is flipping coins.* Only a close look at the public opinion that underlies voting in the knife-edge elections of recent years can provide the correct interpretation. As Chapters 3–6 report, public opinion data reveal an electorate much closer to the picture in the bottom panel of Figure 2.1 than to the top panel.

CONTRIBUTING FACTOR #2.
POLITICAL ACTIVISTS ARE NOT
NORMAL PEOPLE

Here we use the term "normal" in the descriptive sense of "typical" or "representative."[3] For at least a half century public opinion analysts have contrasted political "elites" with the "mass public," terms which seem somewhat antiquated today. For the most part we will use the summary term "political class" to describe the collection of officeholders, party and issue activists, interest group leaders, and political infotainers who constitute the public face of politics in contemporary America. The overwhelming majority of Americans does not fall into these categories and therefore constitutes the "normal" category.

There is no question that the political class *is* polarized, probably genuinely in most cases, but perhaps only tactically in the case of some candidates seeking votes, interest group leaders prospecting for members and money, and infotainers competing for ratings. Polarization of the top political echelons has been widely recognized by political scientists for a half century—at least since the seminal study of 1956 national convention delegates by McCloskey, Hoffman, and O'Hara.[4] We will say more about this subject in Chapters 9 and 10, but for now consider some recent data.

For the past two decades the *New York Times* and *CBS News* have conducted parallel surveys of delegates to the presidential nominating conventions along with representative national sam-

---

3 In Chapter 10 we suggest that political activists are abnormal in other senses as well.
4 Herbert McCloskey, Paul Hoffman, and Rosemary O'Hara. "Issue Conflict and Consensus Among Party Leaders and Followers," *American Political Science Review* 54 (1960): 406–427.

TABLE 2.1
Party Activists are More Extreme than Partisan Identifiers

	DELEGATE DIFFERENCE	IDENTIFIER DIFFERENCE
Government should do more to solve national problems	72	13
Cut taxes to improve economy	67	35
Make all or most tax cuts permanent	88	35
Abortion should be generally available	62	32
New anti-terrorism laws excessively restrict civil liberties	62	28
Extremely important to work through UN	72	35
No legal recognition of gay relationships	44	19
Government should do more to promote traditional values	40	35

ples. These surveys permit comparisons between the responses of high-level party activists on the one hand, and normal Republicans and Democrats in the population as a whole on the other. Table 2.1 reports a selection of responses to the 2004 surveys, responses that reflect the typical pattern over the past quarter-century. Republican and Democratic delegates are an incredible 72 percentage points apart on the general subject of active government whereas party identifiers in the larger population are only 13 points apart. Differences on specific issues are not as huge as this, but they are generally twice as large for the delegates as for the party identifiers. This pattern of polarized partisan activists contrasted with far less polarized partisan identifiers is a general one across time and probably even across countries.

Has the political class become even *more* polarized over the years? We cannot answer that question using surveys like those of the NYT/CBS because the questions they include change from year to year,[5] but other data suggest that the answer is yes. Campaign activists in the national election studies have become somewhat more polarized over the past three decades, reflecting the partisan sorting that we will discuss in Chapter 4.[6] And one highly specific category of party activists which we can track over time—members of Congress—shows clear evidence of increasing polarization.

Following the lead of psychometricians, political scientists have constructed various scaling methods that in practice turn out to produce very similar results. The current industry standard was developed by Poole and Rosenthal. After scaling all contested House and Senate roll call votes since the beginning of the Republic, they report that for most of U.S. history one dimension suffices to reproduce the observed patterns of roll call votes.[7] In contrast to the relatively centrist mid-century decades Congress shows clear indications of increased polarization in recent decades.[8] For example, Figure 2.2 (after p. 14) contrasts the 1961–62 House of Representa-

---

[5] Between 1988 and 2004 the NYT/CBS survey included a question on ideological self-placement. The responses show no trend (Democratic delegates were most liberal in 2004, Republican delegates most conservative in 1988). On average, Republican delegates were twice as likely to choose the label "very conservative" as Democratic delegates were to choose the label "very liberal."

[6] E.g., Kyle Saunders and Alan Abramowitz, "Ideological Realignment and Active Partisans in the American Electorate," *American Politics Research* 32 (2004): 304. Campaign activists are defined as those who report performing a specified number of campaign activities. This contrasts with someone classified as an activist by virtue of their holding an official party position such as county chair or convention delegate. Both groups have been the subject of research and obviously the two categories overlap.

[7] Keith Poole and Howard Rosenthal, Congress: *A Political-Economic History of Roll Call Voting* (New York: Oxford, 1997). Poole and Rosenthal interpret the dimension as economic liberalism, although the actual content of that dimension varies over time (e.g., silver coinage is not an issue today, although it was in the late nineteenth century). Periodically a second dimension (which appears to be race) emerges as significant, although still of secondary importance relative to the principal economic dimension.

[8] The increased polarization reflects both replacement of moderate members by more extreme ones and moderate members becoming more extreme. See Richard Fleisher and John Bond, "The Shrinking Middle in the US Congress," *British Journal of Political Science* 34 (2004): 429–451. Noteworthy as they are, contemporary polarization levels still fall short of those found in the late nineteenth century. See David Brady and Hahrie Han, "An Extended Historical View of Congressional Party Polarization," paper presented at the Princeton University Conference on the Polarization of American Politics: Myth or Reality? 2004.

tives with the 2001–02 House. The earlier figure shows quite a bit of overlap—by their recorded votes some (blue) Democrats and (red) Republicans position themselves in the central portion of the scale. But by the contemporary era there is almost no overlap—moderates have greatly declined in number and Democrats and Republicans are a breed apart. The pattern for Senate voting is similar.

In sum, what we call the political class in America definitely is polarized and probably has become more so in recent decades. But as the quotation that leads off this book asserts, it is a mistake to assume that what is true of a fraction of Americans who are politically active also holds true for the great preponderance of us. In general, normal Americans are busy earning their livings and raising their families. They are not very well-informed about politics and public affairs, do not care a great deal about politics, do not hold many of their views very strongly, and are not ideological.[9] In contrast, members of the political class are well-informed, care a great deal, have strong views, and are ideological. Moreover, and importantly, they have more extreme views than normal people.

The numbers in Table 2.2 provide some perspective. There are approximately 200 million Americans legally eligible to vote. About 80 million of them did not bother to vote in the exceptionally high-turnout 2004 election.

Michael Moore's *Fahrenheit 9/11* was seen by approximately 18 million people. If every person who saw the movie was an eligible

---

[9] The *locus classicus* is Philip Converse, "The Nature of Belief Systems in Mass Publics," in *Ideology and Discontent*, ed. David Apter (New York: Free Press, 1964): 206–261. After four decades of controversy, Converse's 1960s portrait still holds up pretty well. Indeed, despite the proliferation of information sources in recent decades, research indicates that Americans today are no better-informed (and are perhaps less well-informed) than they were several decades ago. Apparently, the proliferation of new media has given some people easy opportunities to avoid what they could not avoid several decades ago, e.g., gavel-to-gavel network convention coverage. See Michael Delli Carpini and Scott Keeter, *What Americans Know About Politics and Why It Matters* (New Haven: Yale U.P., 1996).

TABLE 2.2
Some Perspective

202 million—eligible voting age population

122 million—voted in 2004

62 million—Bush voters

59 million—Kerry voters

17–18 million—people saw *Fahrenheit 9/11*

15–16 million—people listened to Rush Limbaugh last week

3.3 million—daily audience for *The O'Reilly Factor*

3.3 million—daily audience for *Fox News*

.74 million—2004 Kerry vote in Iowa

.12 million—2004 turnout in Iowa Democratic Caucus

.6 million—Howard Dean's e-mail list

.56 million—number of admitted ferret owners

voter, agreed whole-heartedly with the sentiments expressed in the movie, and voted for Kerry, they would constitute less than one-third of his vote. In a given week perhaps 16 million people hear Rush Limbaugh. If every person who heard him was an eligible voter, agreed completely with Limbaugh, and voted for Bush, they would comprise about one-quarter of his vote.[10]

For all the influence attributed to *Fox News*, on a good day its audience is about 3.3 million—less than 3 percent of those who voted in 2004. *The O'Reilly Factor* has an audience of similar size. If every one of *Fox's* viewers was an eligible voter and voted

---

[10] In August of 2004 after a massive Annenberg Survey reported that only 8 percent of Americans had seen *Fahrenheit 9/11* and only 7 percent had heard Rush Limbaugh in the previous week, we received a number of calls from journalists who were incredulous that the numbers were so small given the amount of hype that Moore and Limbaugh receive. National Annenberg Election Survey press release, August 3, 2004.

for George W. Bush, they would make up about 5 percent of his total. In light of such numbers, liberal Democrats' preoccupation with *Fox* seems a touch paranoid.

Five out of six Iowans who voted for John Kerry in November did *not* participate in the spring caucuses when Democratic turnout was at an all-time high. And what about the so-called transformation of American politics by Howard Dean's use of the Internet? His vaunted e-mail list of supporters contained almost 600,000 people, roughly 1 percent of the people who voted for Kerry, and about as many Americans as own ferrets.[11]

Figures like these suggest that there is little or no relationship between the attention paid to the political class in the media and the number of people included. Thousands—even hundreds of thousands—of members of the political class still constitute only a tiny slice of America.

CONTRIBUTING FACTOR #3.
THE MEDIA

Few of the journalists who cover national politics spend much of their time hanging out at big box stores, supermarket chains, or auto parts stores talking to normal people. Rather, they spend most of their time talking to members of the political class and to each other. When they do leave the politicized salons of Washington, New York, and Los Angeles, they do so mainly to cover important political events which are largely attended by members

---

[11] Brendan Koerner, "Feeding the Beast (Or at Least the Ferret)," *New York Times*, January 9, 2005, Section C2. Given that ferret ownership is illegal in some populous jurisdictions such as the state of California and New York City, the figure is surely an underestimate—the odds that a randomly chosen voter was on Dean's e-mail list probably are lower than the odds that he or she owns a ferret.

of the political class. Thus, journalists tend to be greatly over-exposed to a slice of America that is not at all representative. The political class that journalists talk to and observe is polarized, but the people who comprise it are not typical.

Biased exposure naturally leads journalists to portray the unrepresentative as representative. That tendency is reinforced by prevailing news values. While popular media criticism pays a great deal of attention to questions of partisan and ideological bias, academic critics worry as much or more about biases arising from news values—what constitutes news in the eyes of those who make the decisions about what gets printed and shown. Novelty and negativity are two characteristics that enhance news value. Another is conflict. "New survey shows Americans agree on most things—details at 11:00" is not the kind of teaser likely to induce people to stay up and watch the news. "Democrats and Republicans similar on most issues" is not the kind of headline likely to capture the attention of newspaper or magazine readers. In contrast, stories that can be framed in terms of battles and wars, victories and defeats, unbridgeable gulfs and irreconcilable differences are more attractive, especially if they portend even more serious consequences—splits, disruption, even (hopefully?) violence.

For example, consider an extensive follow-up report on the 2000 elections published in *USA Today*.[12] The newspaper selected two towns—Montclair, New Jersey and Franklin, Tennessee—to exemplify the political differences widely assumed to exist between the red and blue states. The three-day report discussed public opinion in the towns along with detailed reporting on the residents and

---

[12] "One Nation, divided," *USA Today*, February 18–20, 2002. The articles are reprinted as a Special Report available at www.usatodaycollege.com.

their views. The resulting profile painted a vivid portrait of a deeply divided America.

Montclair, where Gore got three-quarters of the vote, is described as a bustling suburb. With jazz clubs, art museums, and coffee bars it is "teeming with energy and interaction." According to the profile, the local interest groups and associations are prominently left of center: "Montclair has its own gun control, abortion rights, and anti-war groups, its own chapters of Amnesty International and the NAACP." The Council for Secular Humanism recently opened up a "faith-free" Center for Inquiry.[13]

In contrast, Franklin, Tennessee, where Bush won by almost thirty points, has brick buildings on Main Street and "shops with such names as Pigg & Peach and Heart and Hands." A Confederate war memorial stands on the town square. The Christian music industry is prominent, and the Gospel Music Association is looking for space in the town. Franklin's interest groups and associations are right-leaning: "It's home to the Middle Tennessee Home Education Association for home-schoolers and Christian World Broadcasting, which produces Christian programming in Russian and Chinese and beams it to those countries from a tower in Alaska." The local colleges are mostly Christian.[14]

USA Today went to some length to highlight differences between the two towns. On gun control, for example, *USA Today* interviewed a gun control activist in Montclair, the father of a young man left permanently crippled by a Palestinian terrorist in a 1997 shooting on the Empire State Building observation deck. His

13 Jill Lawrence, "Values, votes, points of view separate towns—and nation," *USA Today*, February 18, 2002: 6.
14 Jill Lawrence, "One nation, divided" *USA Today*, February 18, 2002: 7.

views were contrasted with the views of the owner of the Franklin Gun Shop.[15] In all likelihood readers remember vivid contrasts like these—however extreme and unrepresentative—much longer than small differences in nationally representative polls, such as those we report in the following chapters.

The 2004 campaign provided similar examples of the media's infatuation with the polarization frame. A series of articles in the *Washington Post* described the (purported) "growing consensus of political scientists, demographers and strategists" that "American politics appears to be hardening into uncompromising camps."[16] One article reported from Sugar Land, Texas, prominently featuring one Britton Stein:

> *He lives in a house that has six guns in the closets and 21 crosses in the main hallway. His wife cuts his hair with electric clippers. His three daughters aren't embarrassed when he kisses them on their cheeks. He loves his family, hamburger and his dog. He believes in God, prays daily and goes to church weekly. He has a jumbo smoker in his back yard and a 40-foot tree he has climbed to hang Christmas lights. He has a pickup truck that he has filled with water for the Fourth of July parade, driving splashing kids around a community where Boy Scouts plant American flags in the yards. His truck is a Chevy. His beer is Bud Light. His savior is Jesus Christ. His neighbors include Rep. Tom DeLay (R-Tex.) the House majority leader . . .[17]*

---

[15] Jill Lawrence, "Towns on opposite sides of gun debate," *USA Today*, February 19: 8–9.

[16] David Von Drehle, "Political Split is Pervasive," www.washingtonpost.com, April 25, 2004.

[17] David Finkel, "For a Conservative, Life is Sweet in Sugar Land, Tex.," www.washingtonpost.com, April 26, 2004.

Having intimated that Mr. Stein is a representative Bush voter, the *Post* next sent a reporter to San Francisco in search of typical Kerry voters:

> *Tom Harrison, 62, is a union official. Maryanne Harrison, 60, runs an after-school program. Heather Harrison, 29, is a teacher. Matthew Harrison, 28, is an electrician. . . . Their neighborhood is filled with restaurants that are cafes, and stores that are boutiques, and their neighbors include straight people, gay people, rich people, homeless people, married people, single people, and the House minority leader, Rep. Nancy Pelosi (D-Calif.) . . . .*[18]

In sum, rather than draw the conclusion that America has split into two distinct camps from a systematic look at a broad array of data, the media often reverse the process, selecting unusual but colorful examples to fit the prior conclusion that the country is deeply split.

CONTRIBUTING FACTOR #4.
CONFUSING POSITIONS WITH CHOICES

Another factor contributing to the misperception that the country is deeply divided is the failure to distinguish between peoples' positions and their choices.[19] Some readers considered the data reported in the first edition of this book, and had a reaction

---

[18] David Finkel, "A Liberal Life in the City by the Bay," www.washingtonpost.com, April 27, 2004.
[19] This confusion underlies much of the critique of our argument by Alan Abramowitz and Kyle Saunders, "Why Can't We All Just Get Along? The Reality of a Polarized America," 3(2005). www.bepress.com/forum/vol3/iss2/art1/.

along the following lines: "Okay, the data you report show what you say, but what about other data? What about polls showing that 90 percent of Republicans are going to vote for Bush and 90 percent of Democrats are going to vote for Kerry? Isn't that polarization?"

Indeed, it is, but it is polarization of people's *choices,* not polarization of their *positions.* When we say that Americans are not particularly polarized today, nor discernibly more polarized than they were a few decades ago, we are referring to the policy positions they hold. But a voter's choice of whom to vote for depends not only on his or her position, but also on the positions of the candidates between whom he or she is choosing. If *our* positions have not polarized but our choices have, the implication is that *their* positions have polarized.

Before illustrating how candidate polarization polarizes voter choices, it is worthwhile to point out that polarized Republican choices are nothing new. Figure 2.3 plots the percentage of self-identified Republicans (Democrats) who reported voting for the Republican (Democratic) presidential candidate in the elections between 1952 and 2004.[20] In 2004 Republicans did support George W. Bush a bit more solidly than they supported his father in 1988 and 1992 and Robert Dole in 1996. But Republican support for George W. Bush was about the same as for Dwight Eisenhower in 1952 and 1956, Richard Nixon in 1968 and 1972, and Ronald Reagan in 1980 and 1984. Republicans contributed nothing to increased polarization of vote choices in 2004; rather, the increase reflected the fact that Democrats have begun to look

---

[20] Party categories include those who identified strongly and those who identified less strongly.

FIGURE 2.3

Republican Percent of Two-Party Presidential Vote: 1952–2004

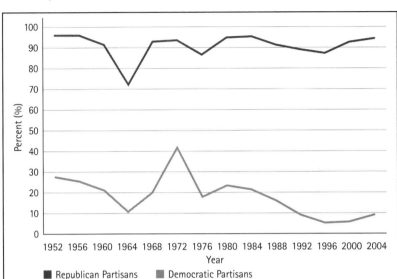

Source: The National Election Studies.
Note: Party identification includes strong and weak partisans.

more like Republicans when it comes to delivering solid support for their candidates.[21]

To see how candidate polarization can polarize voter choices, consider Figure 2.4 (after p. 14). The figure is an idealized comparison of the electoral choice at mid-century when no one was talking much about a polarized America, and today, when many people are.[22] We assume that Democrats (blue) are on the left side of the spectrum, some more liberal, some more conservative, with

---

[21] The decline in white southern Democrats accounts for some of this change, of course, but by no means most of it. The Democrats have shed conservative and moderate identifiers across the country, leaving the party more liberal and more homogeneous (and smaller).

[22] At mid-century a common complaint was that there wasn't "a dime's worth of difference between the parties," reflecting primarily the Republican adoption of "me-too" politics.

a central tendency at the peak of the blue triangle. Republican positions are analogous, only on the right side of the spectrum, with a central tendency at the peak of the red triangle. Independents constitute the gray triangle between the two parties.

At mid-century the received political wisdom was that parties should nominate candidates on the moderate side of their party who might appeal to the uncommitted or independent voter. In their hearts most Democratic activists probably preferred Adlai Stevenson in 1960, but having lost twice with him they nominated John Kennedy, a more conservative Democrat. For their part, after a long losing streak Republicans passed over true conservative Robert Taft in 1952 and nominated moderate "modern Republican" Dwight Eisenhower.

Today, the traditional wisdom has less of a hold on parties. In 2000 Al Gore eschewed Bill Clinton's electorally successful strategy of "triangulation" (positioning himself between Congressional Democrats and Republicans) and emphasized policies that appealed more specifically to the Democratic base. And in 2004 reams of copy were written about Karl Rove's strategy of mobilizing the Republican base.[23]

For purposes of argument assume that voters are fixed—they do not change their positions at all.[24] Now, consider the reaction of voters when the candidates change from "centrist" to "base" strategies. As Democratic candidates move left, conservative Democrats will like them somewhat less, but any reduction in

---

[23] E.g., Ronald Brownstein, "Bush Aims to Solidify His Base," www.latimes.com, August 22, 2004. John Harris, "Once Again, targeting the base works for Bush," www.MSNBC.com, November 3, 2004.

[24] Of course, we do not believe that voters and issues are exactly the same as they were forty years ago—as we discuss in the next chapter there is clearly an ongoing process of party sorting. But the purpose of the example is to show that voter choices can polarize even if voter positions do not change in any way.

their support will be more than offset by the candidate's having moved closer to a greater proportion of their party who now like them more.[25] Even more importantly, the Democratic candidate will now be farther from *every single Republican*. Hence, more Democrats will like their candidate better and all Republicans will like the Democratic candidate less. The situation is symmetrical for Republicans. As Republican candidates move to the right, liberal Republicans like them less but more of their own partisans like them better *and every single Democrat likes them less*. Meanwhile independents will be farther from both parties' candidates and in consequence may be less likely to vote at all.[26] The combined effect is polarization of voter choices—somewhat more enthusiastic support of partisans for their own candidates coupled with more intense opposition to the other party's candidates, and lower turnout among moderates. And this increased polarization of electoral choices results entirely from movement by the candidates, not the voters, who by assumption stayed exactly the same.

This is an appropriate place to clear up another common misconception in recent political commentary. During the 2004 campaign there were numerous claims that swing voters had disappeared.[27] The parties, especially the Republicans, were concentrating their efforts on the base because nearly all Americans were firmly committed—there were no undecideds left to persuade. In the narrow sense this claim was true—in the 2004 race between

---

[25] Providing, of course, that they don't move too far and overshoot the central tendency of the party.

[26] The much discussed decline in presidential turnout from 1960–2000 was entirely due to reduced turnout among moderates and independents. Turnout among the most partisan and ideological Americans never declined. See Morris Fiorina, "Parties, Participation, and Representation in America: Old Theories Face New Realities," in Ira Katznelson and Helen Milner, eds., *Political Science: The State of the Discipline* (New York: Norton, 2002), 537–38.

[27] As low as 5 percent according to some pollsters, as high as 20 percent with weaker definitions. See John Cochran, "Democrats Polish Message, Renew Push for Swing Voters," *CQ Weekly*, July 31, 2004: 1857.

Bush and Kerry there were fewer swing voters than usual. But voters are not born committed or uncommitted; they are made so by the choices they are offered. Consider that in 2004 seven of the top eight Kerry states had Republican governors, while nine states that Bush carried by double-digit margins had Democratic governors. In all, 21 states cast their presidential votes for the party opposite their sitting governor.

Such partisan inconsistency could arise from off-year to on-year changes in turnout of course, but no such excuse is available to explain Montana in 2004.[28] George W. Bush carried the state by 20 points and Montanans passed a gay marriage prohibition by a 67:33 margin. At the same time they were casting these bright red votes, Montanans elected a Democratic governor and turned control of the state Senate over to the Democrats. To further confound any description of the state's color they approved a medical marijuana initiative by almost as large a margin as the gay marriage prohibition. Evidently quite a few Montanans were comfortable swinging from red to blue depending on the choices they were offered.

Finally, consider the following thought experiment. If, by some strange turn of events, Senator John McCain had been the Republican nominee and Senator Joseph Lieberman the Democrat in 2004, would we have seen 90 percent of each party opposing 90 percent of the other? We think not. Candidates viewed as less extreme and less partisan then Kerry and Bush would have produced more swing voters. Some evidence consistent with this argument came from a poll conducted in June 2004 when there was a rumor that Kerry had offered the Democratic vice-presidential nomination to McCain. At a time when nearly all voters were sup-

---

[28] Walter Kirn, "What Color is Montana?" nytimes.com, January 2, 2005.

posedly committed to one candidate or the other, Kerry went up 14 percentage points in a trial heat that offered voters a Kerry-McCain ticket.[29]

An analogous argument explains the growing partisan polarization of presidential approval ratings. As illustrated by Figure 2.5, in 2004 nearly 90 percent of Republicans approved of George W. Bush's performance as president while nearly 90 percent of Democrats disapproved, the greatest such polarization since the early 1950s.[30] But presidential evaluations do not depend only on voter positions: they depend equally on the president's actions. Imagine if, following the generally popular Afghanistan war, President Bush had governed in a very different manner—not invading Iraq, not pushing through cuts in capital gains and dividend income taxes, not proposing drilling in the Arctic National Wildlife Refuge, not proposing a constitutional amendment to prohibit gay marriage—would evaluations of his performance be as polarized as they are today? We do not think so. Presidential evaluations are polarized not because voter positions are polarized, but because George W. Bush chose courses of action that were polarizing.

In sum, while some people are rock-ribbed partisans who would not vote for the other party's candidate under any circumstances, many people are not committed voters or swing voters in any absolute sense. Rather, they tell the pollsters their mind is made up when their choice is Bush or Kerry. Given different alternatives, many of them would tell the pollsters something different.

---

29 CBS News poll cited in Elisabeth Bumiller, "Bush and McCain, Together, Call Iraq War a Conflict Between Good and Evil," *New York Times International*, June 19, 2004: A6.
30 Jeffrey Jones, "Bush Ratings Show Historical Levels of Polarization," Gallup News Release, June 4, 2004. Gary Jacobson, "The Public, the President, and the War in Iraq," Paper presented at the Annual Meeting of the Midwest Political Science Association, Chicago, IL, April 7–10, 2005.

FIGURE 2.5
Partisan Polarization of Bush Approval

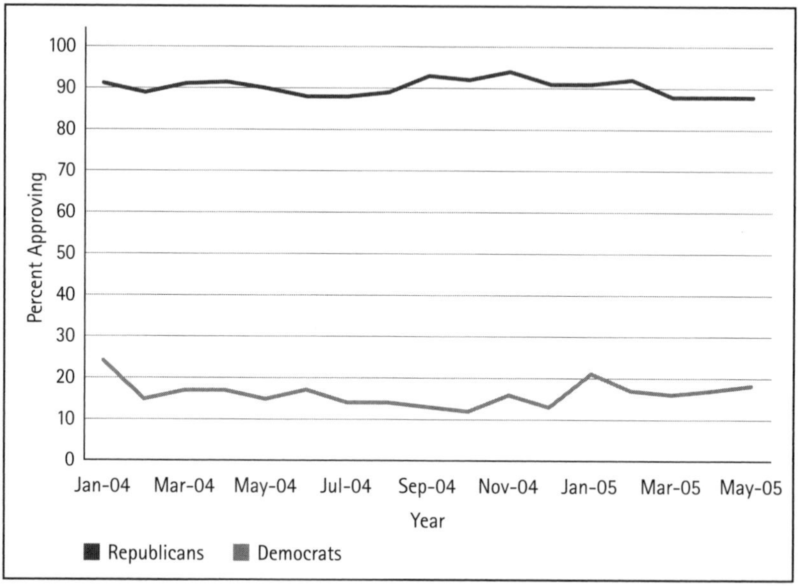

Source: The Gallup Organization.

PREVIEW

In Chapters 7–10 we will return to some of the issues discussed above. In the intervening four chapters we report data that demonstrates that the country at large is not particularly polarized. Public opinion data are far more consistent with the argument that a polarized political class makes voters appear polarized when they are not, than with the argument that a polarized electorate is forcing the political class to take more polarized positions. Widespread impressions to the contrary reflect a combination of the factors discussed in this chapter.

CHAPTER 3

A 50:50 Nation?
Red and Blue State People are
Not That Different

Do we truly believe that ALL red-state residents are ignorant racist fascist knuckle-dragging NASCAR-obsessed cousin-marrying roadkill-eating tobacco-juice-dribbling gun-fondling religious fanatic rednecks; or that ALL blue-state residents are godless unpatriotic pierced-nose Volvo-driving France-loving left-wing communist latte-sucking tofu-chomping holistic-wacko neurotic vegan weenie perverts?[1]

In the immediate aftermath of the 2004 election, some commentators accepted humorist Dave Barry's caricatures as all too true. Understandably, most such reactions came from people on the losing side. *New York Times* columnist Maureen Dowd wrote

---

[1] Dave Barry, "Can't we all just get along?" www.herald.com, December 12, 2004.

that Bush advisor Karl Rove had marshaled "the forces of darkness to take over the country," by appealing to "strains of isolationism, nativism, chauvinism, Puritanism and religious fanaticism."[2] And novelist Jane Smiley's screed circulated widely on the Internet:

> *[Bush and Cheney] . . . know no boundaries or rules. They are predatory and resentful, amoral, avaricious, and arrogant. Lots of Americans like and admire them because lots of Americans, even those who don't share those same qualities, don't know which end is up. . . . red state types love to cheat and intimidate, so we have to assume the worst and call them on it every time.*[3]

IS AMERICA POLARIZED?

Do sentiments like those quoted above bear even a faint resemblance to reality? In the previously quoted words of Matthew Dowd, George W. Bush's chief election strategist in 2004, do 80–90 percent of Americans "look at each other like they are on separate planets?" Happily, the answer is no—Dowd's claim would be closer to the truth had he said "10–20 percent." The public opinion data we report in this chapter show that policy differences among red and blue state residents were far smaller in 2000 and 2004 than generally assumed.

Surprisingly, there have been few such analyses previously, although commentators often present sociological factoids as if

---

2 Maureen Dowd, "Rove's Revenge," *New York Times*, November 7, 2004, nytimes.com.
3 Jane Smiley, "The unteachable ignorance of the red states," slate.msn.com/id/2109218/.

TABLE 3.1
Red Versus Blue State Political Factoids

	RED	BLUE
Born-again?	46%	29%
Born-again and voted for Bush	29	18
Own a gun?	43	30
Own a gun and voted for Bush	28	19

Source: Gun ownership data from 2004 NES; evangelical data from YouGov Internet Survey.

their electoral implications were self-evident. For example, contrasts between the number of gun owners in red and blue states and the number of "born-again" Christians in red and blue states are common.[4] Such sociological differences are real (Table 3.1), but they implicitly invite the reader to assume that they map perfectly on to Democratic and Republican votes. In fact, 37 percent of self-avowed born-again Christians voted Democratic in 2004, so that a 17 percent red-blue difference in the sociological characteristic translated into a smaller 11 percent difference in the vote. Similarly, because 37 percent of gun owners voted for Kerry, a 13 percent red-blue difference in gun ownership translated only into a 9 percent difference in vote. Other sociological characteristics have even weaker translations.

---

[4] Some commentators have pointed out pop culture similarities between red and blue state residents, such as comparable popularity of risqué television shows like *Sex and the City*, and *Queer Eye for the Straight Guy*. The three states where *Playboy Magazine* had its highest rate of readership all voted for Bush in 2004. "Where Playboy and Will and Grace Reign," *New York Times Week in Review*, November 21, 2004: 14.

RED VERSUS BLUE IN 2000[5]

Barely two months before the "values chasm separating the blue states from the red ones" supposedly emerged in the 2000 election, the Pew Research Center for the People & the Press conducted an extensive national survey that included a wide sampling of issues, a number of which figure prominently in discussions of the culture war.[6] We divided the Pew survey respondents into those who resided in states that two months later were to be categorized as blue states and states that two months later were to be categorized as red states. Was there any indication in these data that the election results would leave one-half of the country "seething" and one half "cheering," as *USA Today* reported?

Very little. Table 3.2 indicates that despite the differing political coloration of their states, the residents were not very different. The difference between the proportions of red and blue state respondents who identified themselves as Democrats is not statistically significant, and the difference in the proportions who identified themselves as Republicans is barely so—in both red and blue states self-identified independents were the largest group. Similarly, about a fifth of the respondents in both red and blue states considered themselves liberals (the 4-point difference is not statistically significant), and while there were more conservatives than liberals in the red states, there were more conservatives than liberals even in the blue states. In both red and blue states the largest group of peo-

---

5 This section is a slightly condensed version of the corresponding section in the first edition.

6 The Pew survey was conducted August 24–September 10, 2000. Pew's summaries of the findings (along with links to the data and questionnaires) are contained in two separate reports: "Issues and Continuity Now Working for Gore," www.people-press.org/reports/display.php3?ReportID=33 and "Religion and Politics: The Ambivalent Majority," www.people-press.org/reports/display.php3? ReportID=32.

TABLE 3.2
Red Versus Blue States: Political Inclinations in 2000

	RED	BLUE
Democratic self-ID	32%	36%
Republican self-ID	31	25
Liberal self-ID	18	22
Conservative self-ID	41	33

ple classified themselves as moderates. In sum, while red and blue states would vote for different candidates in November, the underlying patterns of political identification were not very different.

Table 3.3 reports similar results for the group evaluations offered by residents of red and blue states. Unsurprisingly, red state residents viewed the Republican Party more favorably than the Democrats, but 55 percent of them viewed the Democratic Party favorably as well. Conversely, blue state residents regarded the Democratic Party more favorably than the Republicans, but 50 percent reported favorable evaluations of the Republican Party. Evangelical Christians were evaluated equally positively by solid majorities in both red and blue states, as were Jews and Catholics. Muslims fared less well overall and red state residents regarded them lower still, but this was 2000, when the concept of a Muslim was pretty abstract to most Americans, especially in the red states. Finally, neither red nor blue state residents liked atheists. This is a standard finding: Americans do not care very much what or how people believe, as long as they believe in something.[7]

---

[7] As President-elect Dwight Eisenhower stated in a 1952 address, "our form of government has no sense unless it is founded in a deeply religious faith, and I don't care what it is."

TABLE 3.3

Red Versus Blue States: Group Evaluations in 2000
(Percent very/mostly favorable toward . . .)

	RED	BLUE
Republican Party	58%	50%
Democratic Party	55	64
Evangelical Christians	63	60
Jews	77	79
Catholics	79	77
Muslims	47	56
Atheists	27	37

Across a range of other matters, blue and red state residents differed little, if at all. Figures in Table 3.4 indicate that similar proportions viewed the government as *almost always* wasteful and inefficient—relative to the red states, the blue states were not wellsprings of support for big government. Only small minorities in either category considered discrimination as the main reason that African Americans can't get ahead—the blue states were not hotbeds of racial liberalism. Immigrants received a warmer reception among blue state residents, but multiculturalism remained a minority position even in the blue states. Blue state residents were less likely to endorse unqualified patriotism.

On the other hand, red state residents were just as likely as blue state residents to believe that large companies have too much power and to think that corporations make too much profit—the red states were not the running dogs of corporate America. Amusingly, majorities in both red and blue states agreed that Al Gore was more of a liberal than he let on, and that George Bush was more of

TABLE 3.4
Red Versus Blue States: Beliefs and Perceptions in 2000
(Percent strongly supporting statement)

	RED	BLUE
Gov't almost always wasteful and inefficient	44%	39%
Discrimination main reason blacks cannot get ahead	21	25
Immigrants strengthen our country	32	44
Fight for country right or wrong	43	35
Too much power concentrated in large companies	62	64
Corporations make too much profit	43	44
Al Gore is more liberal than he lets on	59	55
George Bush is more conservative than he lets on	57	59
Wish Clinton could run again (strongly disagree)	61	51

a conservative than he let on—they were not fooled by all the verbiage about "progressives" and "compassionate conservatives." Finally—and counter to suggestions of numerous Democrats after the election—majorities in both red and blue states *strongly* disagreed with the proposition that they wish Bill Clinton could run again. Clinton was more favorably regarded in the blue states, but Clinton fatigue by no means was limited to the red states.

When it comes to issue sentiments, Table 3.5 shows that in many cases the small differences we have seen so far became even smaller. Contrary to Republican dogma, red state citizens were equally as unenthusiastic about using the budget surplus (har!) to cut taxes as blue state citizens. Instead, nearly equal numbers of blue and red state residents thought the surplus should have been used to pay off the national debt, increase domestic spending, and bolster Social Security and Medicare. Contrary to Democratic

TABLE 3.5
Red Versus Blue States: Issue Sentiments in 2000

	RED	BLUE
Should use the surplus to cut taxes	14%	14%
. . . pay off the national debt	23	21
. . . increase domestic spending	24	28
. . . bolster SS and Medicare	38	35
Favor abolition of inheritance tax	72	70
. . . gov't grants to religious organizations	66	67
. . . school vouchers for low and middle-income parents	50	54
. . . partial privatization of SS	71	69
. . . Medicare coverage of prescription drugs	92	91
. . . increasing defense spending	37	30
Do whatever it takes to protect the environment	64	70

dogma, blue state citizens were equally as enthusiastic as red state citizens about abolishing the inheritance tax, giving government grants to religious organizations, adopting school vouchers, and partially privatizing Social Security. Overwhelming majorities in both red and blue states favored Medicare coverage of prescription drugs, and solid majorities endorsed protecting the environment, whatever it takes. Neither red nor blue state residents attached high priority to increasing defense spending. Looking at this series of issue items, one wonders why anyone would bother separating respondents into red and blue categories—the differences are mostly insignificant.

But, we have not considered the specific issues that most clearly define the culture war. Table 3.6 brings us to the heart of

TABLE 3.6
Red Versus Blue States: Religion and Moral Views in 2000

	RED	BLUE
Religion is very important in my life	74%	62%
Churches should keep out of politics	43	46
Is it ever right for clergy to discuss candidates or issues from the pulpit? (yes)	33	35
Ban dangerous books from school libraries (yes)	42	37
Homosexuality should be accepted by society		
Agree strongly	31	41
Agree not strongly	14	16

the matter—questions of religion, morality, and sexuality.[8] A higher proportion of red state respondents claimed that religion is very important in their lives, but a healthy 62 percent majority of blue state respondents felt the same. Very similar proportions thought churches should stay out of politics, and the minority of red state residents who approve of the clergy talking politics from the pulpit was a bit smaller than the minority in the blue states who approved. Book-burners were only slightly more common in the red states. Finally, there was a clear difference in one of the major issues of the culture war, homosexuality, but probably less of a difference than many would have expected. The level of support for societal acceptance of homosexuality was 10 percentage points higher in the blue states (it grows to 12 points if we add those who waffle to those who fully accept homosexuality). The

[8] Unfortunately, there was no question about abortion views in the Pew Survey, only an item on "which party would better represent your views?" Such items are contaminated by projection and rationalization. We deal with the question of abortion at length in chapter 4.

difference is statistically significant, but it hardly conjures up an image of two coalitions of deeply opposed states engaged in a culture war. Opinion was almost as divided within the red and the blue states as it was between them. Significantly, the 10- to 12-point difference on the issue of homosexual acceptance is as large a difference as we found between red and blue state respondents in the survey. Readers can judge for themselves whether differences of this magnitude justify the military metaphors usually used to describe them.

A natural objection to the preceding comparisons is that they include all citizens rather than just voters. Barely more than half of the age-eligible electorate went to the polls in 2000, and it is well known that partisanship and ideology are correlates of who votes: more intense partisans and more extreme ideologues are more likely to vote.[9] Thus, it is possible that the *voters* in red states differ more from the *voters* in blue states than the residents do. To consider this possibility we turned to the 2000 National Election Study which—after the election—asks individuals whether and how they voted.[10]

Tables 3.7 and 3.8 report differences among reported voters in the NES that are only marginally larger than those reported among all respondents in the Pew Survey. Self-identified Democrats were significantly more common among blue state voters and self-identified Republicans significantly more common among

---

9 For time series data see Figures 2a–2b and 3a–3b in Morris Fiorina, "Whatever Happened to the Median Voter?" available at www.stanford.edu/~mfiorina/.
10 www.umich.edu/~nes/. The National Election Studies is a research and data-distribution organization located at the University of Michigan and supported by the National Science Foundation. Surveys have been conducted in every national election year since 1952. The NES is not responsible for our analyses or interpretations of the data they distribute.

TABLE 3.7
Red Versus Blue States: Political Inclinations in 2000

	RED	BLUE
Democratic self-ID*	32%	40%
Republican self-ID	34	25
Liberal self-ID	11	20
Conservative self-ID	31	24
Prefer unified control	24	24

* Party identifiers include strong and weak identifiers, not independent leaners.
Liberal identifiers are scale positions 1–2, conservative identifiers 6–7.

red state voters, but in neither case does the difference reach double digits; independents and minor party affiliates were a third of the actual electorate in both categories. Self-identified liberals were more common in the blue states, but self-identified conservatives were at least as numerous as liberals in blue states.[11] A plurality of voters in both red and blue states placed themselves in the exact center of the NES liberal-conservative scale. Finally, rather than blue state residents longing for Democratic control of both the Presidency and the Congress and red state residents longing for Republican control of both, nearly identical majorities of both preferred divided party control.

Table 3.8 indicates that issue preferences in the two categories of states were surprisingly similar in many instances. Four in ten voters in both red and blue states agreed that immigration should decrease, and seven in ten believed that English should be the

---

[11] The NES uses a seven-point scale to measure ideology. We classify liberals (conservatives) as people who place themselves in the two left (right) most positions: extremely liberal (conservative) and liberal (conservative). The three center positions are slightly liberal, middle-of-the-road, slightly conservative.

TABLE 3.8
Red Versus Blue State Voters: Issue Preferences in 2000

	RED	BLUE
Immigration should decrease*	43%	41%
Make English official language	66	70
Environment over jobs	42	43
Favor school vouchers	54	51
Favor death penalty	77	70
Government should ensure fair treatment of blacks in employment	51	57
Blacks should get preferences in hiring	14	13
Stricter gun control	52	64
Equal women's role**	82	83
Attend church regularly	65	50
Moral climate: much worse	30	26
somewhat worse	25	25
Tolerate others' moral views	62	62
Abortion—always legal	37	48
Allow homosexual adoption	40	52
No gay job discrimination	62	73
Favor gays in military (strongly)	44	60

* Unless otherwise noted, the figures in the table combine "strongly" or "completely agree" responses with "mostly" or "somewhat agree" responses.
** Scale positions 1–2

official language of the United States (the proportion actually was slightly higher in the blue states). Four in ten voters in both categories put environmental considerations above employment considerations, a surprising similarity in light of the image of red states as hotbeds of clear-cutters and blue states as strongholds of tree-huggers. Narrow majorities of voters in both categories supported school vouchers, and large majorities supported the death penalty. Only a slightly larger majority in blue states favored government intervention to ensure fair treatment of African Americans in employment, and virtually identical (small) minorities supported racial preferences in hiring.

Again, when we turn to the specific issues that define the purported culture war, larger differences emerged, but there also were numerous surprises. A solid majority of blue state voters supported stricter gun control laws, but so did a narrow majority of red state voters. Support for women's equality was overwhelming and identical among voters in both categories of states. Similar proportions in both red and blue states believed that the moral climate of the country had deteriorated since 1992, and identical proportions believed that others' moral views should be tolerated. Support for unrestricted abortion was 11 points higher among blue state voters, but such unqualified support fell short of a majority, and more than a third of red state voters offered similarly unqualified support.

The 2000 NES was particularly rich in items tapping people's views about matters related to sexual orientation. Here we find differences between blue and red state voters that are statistically significant, though smaller in magnitude than regular consumers of the news might have expected. A narrow majority of blue state voters would allow homosexuals to adopt children, but so would four in ten red state voters. Solid majorities of voters in both categories supported laws that would ban employment discrimination against gays. Sixty percent of blue state voters fully supported gays in the military, contrasted with 44 percent of red state voters. This 16 percent difference was the single largest disparity we found between the issue preferences of red and blue state voters in 2000. Perhaps Bill Clinton picked the one issue in the realm of sexual orientation that was most likely to create controversy. But the evidence supports the alternative hypothesis that Clinton's 1993 executive order polarized the electorate: according to Gallup, popular support for gays in the military rose through the 1980s and had reached 60 percent in 1989 before plummeting in the wake of Clinton's action.[12]

All in all, the comparison of blue and red state voters in 2000 is similar to the picture reflecting comparisons of all residents of blue and red states. There were numerous similarities between red and blue state voters, some differences, and a few notable differences, but little that called to mind the portrait of a culture war between the states.

RED VERSUS BLUE IN 2004

Only three states changed their political hue between 2000 and 2004: Iowa and New Mexico changed from blue to red, and New Hampshire changed from red to blue. Given that public opinion generally does not change rapidly, the picture should be much the same in 2004 as in 2000. Contrary to much popular commentary, it is.

At the time of this writing, a PEW study comparable to that reported for 2000 had not yet been released, but we can present 2004 NES tables parallel to Tables 3.7 and 3.8. As Table 3.9 shows, the political inclinations of voters in red and blue states changed

---

[12] Alan Young, "Poll Trends—Attitudes Toward Homosexuality," *Public Opinion Quarterly* 61 (1997): 502.

FIGURE 3.4
Both Red and Blue State Residents Are Basically Centrists

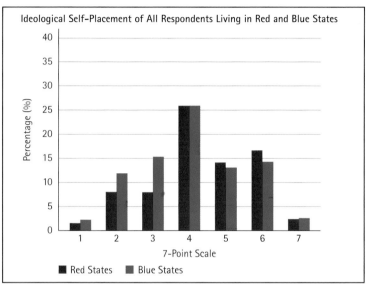

Ideological Self-Placement of All Respondents Living in Red and Blue States

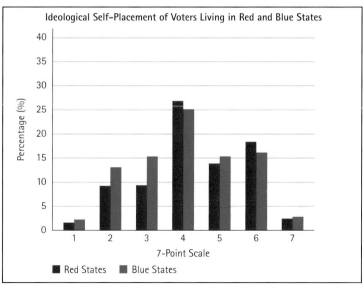

Ideological Self-Placement of Voters Living in Red and Blue States

Source: Calculated from the 2004 National Election Study.

FIGURE 3.5
Both Red and Blue State Voters Agree
that the Parties Are Not Centrist

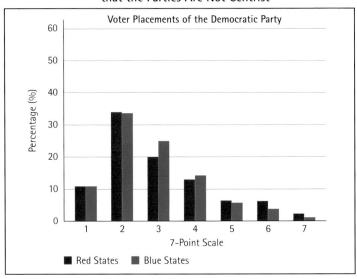

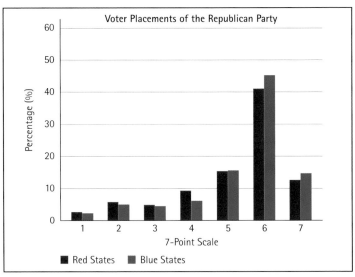

Source: Calculated from the 2004 National Election Study.

TABLE 3.9
Red Versus Blue State Voters: Political Inclinations in 2004

	RED	BLUE
Democratic self-ID*	32%	32%
Republican self-ID	33	25
Liberal self-ID	9	14
Conservative self-ID	22	18
Prefer unified control	22	21

* Party identifiers include strong and weak identifiers, not independent leaners.
Liberal identifiers are scale positions 1–2, conservative identifiers 6–7.

little between 2000 and 2004, and differences between red and blue continue to be minor. Differences in party allegiance are even smaller than in 2000. Democrats are as common in red states as in blue states and Independents continue to be the largest category in both red and blue states. Avowed liberals continue to be scarce in both blue and red states, but avowed conservatives are by no means a majority in red states—pluralities in both red and blue states classify themselves as centrists. Finally, just as was the case in 2000, we do not find a majority of red state voters wishing for unified Republican control of the presidency and Congress and a majority of blue state voters wishing for Democratic control. In both red and blue states only one in five voters shows any enthusiasm for unified party control.

As in 2000, red and blue state voters in 2004 differ little in their evaluations of relevant political groupings (Table 3.10).[13] Since the

---

[13] The group ratings were measured with the NES "thermometer scales." Respondents are asked to give groups a numerical rating where 0 represents the very coldest feeling toward the group, 100 the very warmest, and 50 is neutral.

TABLE 3.10
Red Versus Blue State Voters: Evaluations of Groups in 2004

	RED	BLUE
Democratic Party	59°	58°
Republican Party	56	51
Liberals	55	57
Conservatives	62	59
Christian Fundamentalists	61	53
Jews	68	68
Catholics	68	68
Muslims	54	55
Gay men and lesbians	47	53

Source: 2004 NES.

election Democrats have bemoaned their failure to relate to voters in the red states, but on average red state voters evaluated the Democrats as positively as blue state voters did, and—surprise— red state voters actually evaluated the Democratic Party a bit *more* positively than the Republican Party. Red and blue state voters evaluate liberals virtually identically and red state voters are only a bit more favorable to conservatives than blue state voters. They do not differ in their evaluations of Catholics, Jews, and—in contrast to 2000—even Muslims. Red state voters feel 8 degrees warmer toward Christian Fundamentalists than blue state voters, but even blue state voters rate Fundamentalists a little above the neutral point of the scale. The hysterical Democratic commentators who vilified red state voters after the election clearly overreacted.

Not surprisingly, the issue positions of red and blue state voters differ little in 2004 (Table 3.11). Almost identical pluralities are

TABLE 3.11
Red Versus Blue State Voters: Issue Preferences in 2004

	RED	BLUE
Immigration should decrease*	46%	45%
Environment over jobs**	24	31
Favor school vouchers	34	29
Favor death penalty	72	65
Government should ensure fair treatment of blacks in employment	55	53
Blacks should get preferences in hiring	21	13
Stricter gun control	51	63
Equal women's role**	74	78
Moral Climate: Much worse	18	19
Somewhat worse	26	27
Tolerate others' moral views	60	65
Abortion—always legal	32	44
Allow homosexual adoption	41	57
No gay job discrimination	69	81
Favor gays in military (strongly)	51	60
Allow homosexual marriage	31	39

* Unless otherwise noted, the figures in the table combine "strongly" or "completely agree" with "mostly" or "somewhat agree" responses.
** Scale positions 1–2
Source: 2004 NES.

unhappy with present levels of immigration. Red and blue state voters differ somewhat regarding the trade-off between environmental protection and jobs, although in the less favorable economic climate of 2004 support for the environment dropped considerably in both red and blue states. Support for school vouchers also dropped significantly in both red and blue states, but voters in both continue to show similar levels of support and opposition.

On the death penalty there is a statistically significant difference between red and blue state voters, but a two-thirds majority of blue state voters supports it compared to a three-quarters majority of red state voters.

In both red and blue states majorities of 2004 voters think the government should ensure fair treatment of African Americans in employment, but large majorities in both reject racial preferences in hiring. Red and blue state voters are in similarly high agreement about gender equality—red state voters do not wish to keep women pregnant, barefoot, and in the kitchen as many blue state commentators suppose. Red and blue state residents differ on gun control— support for stricter control is 12 percentage points higher in blue states, although even in red states a majority favors stricter control.

Red and blue state voters are in agreement about the deteriorating moral climate of the country, and solid majorities of both believe in toleration of others' moral views. When we focus specifically on abortion and gay issues we find the kind of differences we found in 2000. Support for unrestricted abortion is 12 points higher in the blue states, but even there it falls short of a majority, and a third of red state voters hold this position as well. Blue state voters are 12 points higher in rejecting job discrimination against gays, but a two-thirds majority of red state voters also takes that position. Support for allowing gays to serve openly in the military is 9 points higher among blue state voters, but half the voters in red states hold that position as well. Only the issue of homosexual adoption finds majorities on opposite sides—a majority of blue state voters would allow such adoptions while a majority of red state voters would not. And only a minority in both red and blue states would allow homosexual marriage.

In sum, while "massive colliding forces" is to some extent a subjective judgment, just as in 2000, any interpretation of the 2004 voting as a manifestation of a culture war between red and blue states rests on the weak underpinnings of 10–12 point differences on a few issues that most Americans did not consider to be very important (more on the latter point in Chapters 6 and 8).

THE WAR IN IRAQ

There was one huge difference between the political context in 2000 and 2004—the importance of the constellation of issues concerning national security, terrorism, and the war in Iraq. After the fall of the Berlin Wall in 1989 international and defense issues slipped off the radar screens of most Americans.[14] Such issues played no role in the 2000 election, but 9/11 brought such issues back to prominence. The national unity that followed the terrorist attacks held through the popularly approved war against the Taliban in Afghanistan, but consensus disintegrated after the Bush Administration launched a war against Iraq. As we will discuss in Chapter 8, the defining issues in the 2004 election were leadership in the war on terrorism and homeland security, in contrast to 2000 when domestic issues and the behavior of Bill Clinton played a larger role.

Red and blue America do not differ much when it comes to their views on how the country should approach foreign affairs.

---

[14] Except for a brief spike coincident with the first Gulf War, the Gallup "most important problems" series finds fewer than 10 percent of Americans mentioning a foreign or defense problem between 1990 and 2000.

FIGURE 3.1
Americans Agree on the Necessity for U.S. Involvement in International Affairs

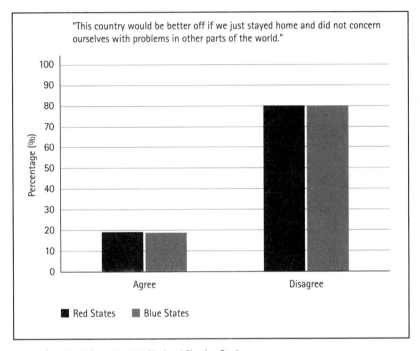

Source: Calculated from the 2004 National Election Study.

As Figure 3.1 shows, they are in complete agreement that the United States must take an active role in international affairs—mid-century Republican isolationism finds as little support in the red states as in the blue states. And while faith in diplomacy versus carrying a big stick is more dispersed, Figure 3.2 indicates that red and blue America differ little in their views, with most tending toward balancing the two.

To be sure, as discussed in Chapter 2 we do find greater differences when we consider evaluations rather than positions. Fig-

FIGURE 3.2
Red and Blue State Voters Have Similar Views
on Diplomacy vs. Force in International Affairs

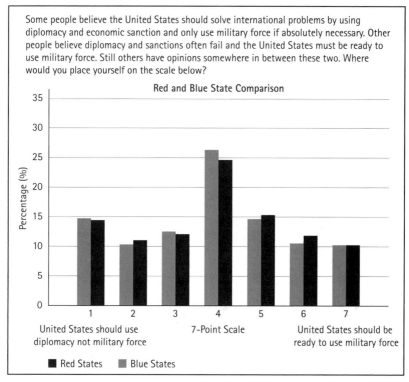

Some people believe the United States should solve international problems by using diplomacy and economic sanction and only use military force if absolutely necessary. Other people believe diplomacy and sanctions often fail and the United States must be ready to use military force. Still others have opinions somewhere in between these two. Where would you place yourself on the scale below?

Red and Blue State Comparison

Percentage (%)

United States should use
diplomacy not military force

7-Point Scale

United States should be
ready to use military force

■ Red States   ■ Blue States

Source: Hillygus and Shields, 2004.

ure 3.3 shows a significant difference between red and blue state residents' evaluations of President Bush's handling of the war in Iraq. But this greater polarization does not stem from differences in voter positions on the issue of war and peace (Figure 3.2); rather, it stems from the relatively extreme policy the president adopted: polarized alternatives make centrist voters look more polarized than they are.

FIGURE 3.3

Americans' Views of What Bush Has Done in Iraq Are More Divided

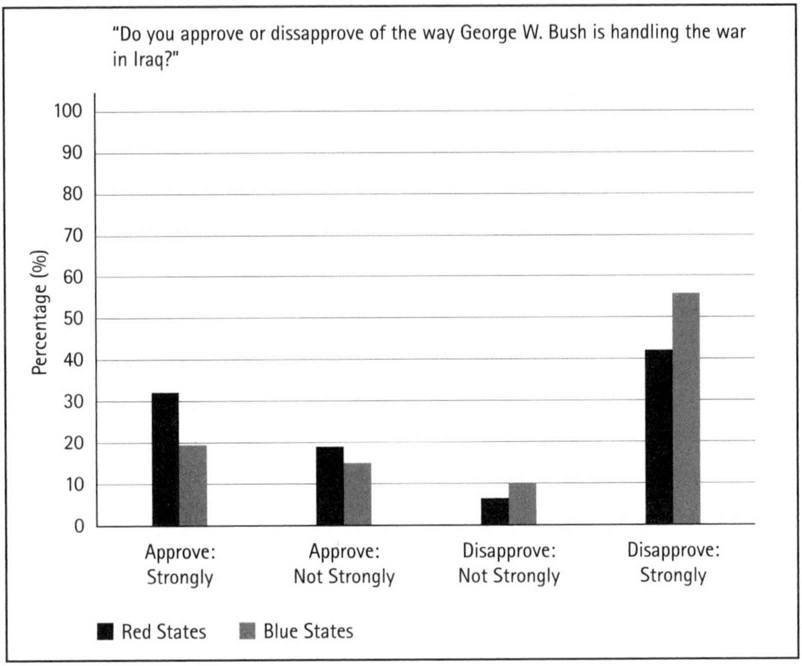
"Do you approve or dissapprove of the way George W. Bush is handling the war in Iraq?"
Percentage (%)
100
90
80
70
60
50
40
30
20
10
0
Approve: Strongly
Approve: Not Strongly
Disapprove: Not Strongly
Disapprove: Strongly
Red States
Blue States

Source: Calculated from the 2004 National Election Study.

RED STATES VERSUS BLUE STATES: A SUMMARY

Since 1972 the National Election Studies have included a question that asks respondents to place themselves on a seven-category liberal-conservative scale that runs from "extremely liberal" on the left to "extremely conservative" on the right. Generally, one-quarter or more of our citizens decline to classify themselves, saying that they don't know what they are or that the terms don't mean anything to them.[15] Figure 3.4 compares the ideological positions of the three-quarters of the people who classify themselves. If the American electorate consisted of "two nations," we would find red state residents overwhelmingly positioned on the right of the scale, and blue state residents overwhelmingly on the left. Instead, we see that the distributions in the red and blue states are similar—both are centered over the "moderate" or "middle-of-the-road" position. Half the voters in both red states and blue states placed themselves in the three center categories in 2004. Combining these moderates with those who do not classify themselves at all, the conclusion is clear: the electorate is largely moderate or ambivalent in its ideological orientation.

Now consider Figure 3.5. Ninety percent of our citizens can place the parties—people are significantly less uncertain about where the parties stand than where they do. Again the distributions in red and blue states are very similar, but in sharp contrast to Figure 3.4, more than 40 percent of voters in both red and blue states place the Democratic Party at the two far left scale positions, and majorities place the Republican Party at the two far right scale positions. In light of the data presented in this chapter we think the evidence is compelling that the bottom panel of Figure 2.1 (after p. 14) better describes the current state of American politics than the top panel. Elections are close, but voters are not deeply or bitterly divided. In both red and blue states a solid majority of voters see themselves as positioned between two relatively extreme parties.

---

[15] Political scientists often add this group to those in the middle scale position, which, of course, would make the case for a centrist electorate even stronger.

Why is the prevailing picture of an America divided into red and blue camps so at odds with a systematic look at public opinion data? As we discussed in Chapter 2, the media tend to pick out colorful but unrepresentative examples to illustrate red and blue state differences. Repeatedly subjected to such "analyses," Americans hardly can be blamed for believing in a culture war between the states. We have read a great deal of popular commentary on the red and blue states, and in our view the journalistic analysis that best reflects the statistical portrait we have painted is contained in David Brooks's sensitive contrast of life in Montgomery County, Maryland, with life in Franklin County, Pennsylvania. Our conclusion mirrors his: "*Although there are some real differences between Red and Blue America, there is no fundamental conflict. There may be cracks, but there is no chasm.*"[16]

---

[16] "One Nation, Slightly Divisible," *The Atlantic*, December 2001: 65.

CHAPTER 4

A 50:50 Nation? Beyond the
Red and the Blue States

Despite the attention the red state/blue state categorization has received in the media, few serious analysts of public opinion would be surprised by the lack of major differences in public opinion between red and blue states. A state is a large aggregation, a gross unit of comparison. California is a blue state, but most of the state's counties are red. Similarly, Texas is a red state, but there is considerable blue in its large cities and along its border with Mexico. For this reason, few professional analysts take the red states/blue states distinction very seriously. Still, one can accept the argument that the division of the country into red and blue is a gross exaggeration but still believe that the country is polarized, increasingly so. We simply need to examine other, more precisely defined categories or dimensions in order to find the expected polarization.

IS THE COUNTRY POLARIZED?
DEMOGRAPHIC AND POLITICAL GROUPS

Happily, we need not bury the reader beneath an avalanche of additional data, for there has been some very thorough research on this subject. DiMaggio, Evans, and Bryson have conducted an intensive analysis of public opinion covering the period 1972 (when the culture war first flared up) through 1994 (when it erupted into the Republican capture of Congress and Bill Clinton's subsequent impeachment). Evans later updated the study through 2002.[1] Their analysis uses data from the National Election Studies (NES) and the General Social Survey (GSS) and focuses squarely on the question of opinion polarization, applying four different statistical measures of polarization to thirty-five different opinion scales.[2] Table 4.1 summarizes their findings.

Contrary to claims of growing polarization, DiMaggio, Evans, and Bryson's exhaustive statistical analysis finds that during the last quarter of the twentieth century older and younger Americans grew more alike in their views, not more dissimilar. So did more-well-educated and less-well-educated Americans, black and white Americans, Americans of different religious denominations, and Americans living in different regions. Despite the appearance of a significant gender gap in post-1980 elections, men and women have become neither more nor less similar than in the early 1970s before the gender gap appeared. Americans who self-classify

[1] Paul DiMaggio, John Evans, and Bethany Bryson, "Have Americans' Social Attitudes Become More Polarized?" *American Journal of Sociology* 102 (1996): 690–775. John Evans, "Have Americans' Attitudes Become More Polarized?—An Update," *Social Science Quarterly* 84 (2003): 71–90.
[2] The NES is described in footnote 10 of chapter 3. The GSS is a continuing study conducted by the National Opinion Research Center at the University of Chicago, partially funded by the National Science Foundation. The survey has been conducted twenty-four times since 1972.

TABLE 4.1
DiMaggio, Evans, and Bryson
Analysis of Opinion Trends

CHANGE IN OPINION OVER TIME?
By Age—convergence
By Education—convergence
By Race—convergence
By Religion—convergence
By Region—convergence
By Gender—no change
By Ideology—no change (except on abortion)
By Party ID—polarization

---

themselves as liberals or conservatives are no further apart now than several decades ago, except on the single issue of abortion. The only category that showed evidence of polarization was self-classification by party affiliation: people who consider themselves Democrats and Republicans are further apart in their views than partisans were several decades ago. Overall, DiMaggio and his coauthors conclude that, "The evidence, then, points to dramatic *depolarization* in intergroup differences" (emphasis in original).

What of the possibility that voters polarized before 1972, the starting point of the DiMaggio, Evans, and Bryson study, but political activists and candidates did not polarize until later? This possibility is inconsistent with evidence that public opinion tends to lag elite behavior not lead it.[3] Moreover, an earlier report by Glenn finds no evidence of increasing polarization between the

---

[3] For example, Edward Carmines and James Stimson, *Issue Evolution* (Princeton, NJ: Princeton University Press, 1989).

early 1950s and late 1960s, although Glenn had fewer measures of opinion available to him than did DiMaggio et al.[4] Ironically, Glenn was searching for evidence of *depolarization* because many at the time thought that the spread of the mass media would have a homogenizing effect on public opinion.

One of the qualifications about the DiMaggio, Evans, and Bryson findings ("no polarization of liberals and conservatives except in the case of abortion") may strike some readers as belonging to the Mrs. Lincoln genre of caveats (Other than that, Mrs. Lincoln, how did you enjoy the play?). If there is a single issue that is the touchstone of the culture war, abortion is it. If there has been significant polarization on abortion, then perhaps it does not matter whether there has been polarization on any other issue. The finding is questioned, however, by Mouw and Sobel who point out that increased polarization on the NES abortion question coincides with a change in question wording.[5] Additionally, they suggest that the meaning of individual responses changed with the change in the status quo made by the Supreme Court's *Webster* decision, concluding that

> *Our results indicate no increase in polarization in abortion attitudes between 1980 and 2000. While the contemporary culture wars have been portrayed as a threat to democratic institutions, our evidence suggests that, at least with respect to the debate over abortion rights, the American public is no more divided now than in the past.*[6]

---

[4] Norval Glenn, "Recent Trends in Intercategory Differences in Attitudes," *Social Forces* 52 (1974): 395–401.
[5] Ted Mouw and Michael Sobel, "Culture Wars and Opinion Polarization: The Case of Abortion," *American Journal of Sociology* 106 (2001): 913–43.
[6] Ibid., 938.

We will leave this subject for now, but we have much more to say about abortion in the next chapter.

PARTISAN POLARIZATION: AKA "SORTING"

The DiMaggio, Evans, and Bryson finding of increasing polarization among self-classified partisans is consistent with previous academic research and is clearly a significant development.[7] But it is crucial to recognize that *partisan* polarization is not the same thing as *popular* polarization. Increasing partisan polarization in the absence of popular polarization indicates that "sorting" has occurred—those who affiliate with a party today are more likely to affiliate with the ideologically "correct" party than they were in earlier periods.[8] Consider Figure 4.1 (see after page 78). The top panel compares two urns which each contain 100 marbles. The urn on the left contains 33 red, 33 blue, and 34 gray marbles. All red marbles bear an R (Republican) stamp, all blues bear a D (Democrat) stamp, and all grays bear an I (Independent) stamp. The urn on the right contains 50 red (R) marbles and 50 blue (D) marbles. This contrast captures what we think most people understand by polarization—the gray "middle" has disappeared and only two distinctly different red and blue categories remain.

---

7 For a recent statement see Jon Bond, "Evidence of Increasing Polarization among Ordinary Citizens," in Jeffrey Cohen, Richard Fleisher, and Paul Kantor, eds., *American Political Parties: Decline or Resurgence* (Washington, DC: CQ Press, 2001): 55–77. Some years ago one of us discussed the significance of this development for electoral position-taking. See Morris Fiorina, "Whatever Happened to the Median Voter?" www.stanford.edu/~mfiorina/.

8 Alan Abramowitz and Kyle Saunders, "Ideological Realignment in the U.S. Electorate," *Journal of Politics* 60 (1998): 634–652.

The bottom panel of Figure 4.1 roughly depicts what has occurred in the United States.[9] Both urns contain 33 red, 33 blue, and 34 gray marbles, and both contain 33 R, 33 D, and 34 I marbles. In these major respects the urns are identical. But there is a difference in the way the marbles are sorted. In the left hand urn 22 of 33 red marbles bear an R stamp and the other 11 bear a D stamp, while 22 of the 33 blue marbles bear a D stamp and the other 11 an R stamp. In the right-hand urn, however, all the red marbles have an R stamp and all the blues have a D stamp. Despite identical proportions of red, blue, gray, R, D, and I marbles in the two urns, the marbles in the urn on the right are more cleanly sorted out than those in the urn on the left. Something like this has happened in the United States over the past few decades.

As is widely appreciated, liberal Republicans (blue R marbles) and conservative Democrats (red D marbles) have declined in number. Blue and red now line up more closely with R and D. The realignment of the South has a lot to do with this, of course. People who once were conservative southern Democrats are now more likely to be conservative southern Republicans, leaving the remaining Democrats more liberal on average and contributing to the increasing conservatism of the Republican Party. But the South is not the entire story.[10] As for the mechanisms underlying these changes, research indicates that to some extent young voters are entering the party consistent with their views and to some extent

---

[9] From about 1984 to the present. If we go back farther in time, to, say, the mid-1960s, there has been a doubling in the proportion of I marbles, and a decline in the proportion of D marbles.

[10] Matt Levendusky, "Sorting in the U.S. Mass Electorate," Paper presented at the 2005 Annual Meetings of the Midwest Political Science Association, Chicago, IL, April 7–9.

people are changing their views to make them consistent with their party affiliation.[11]

Sorting is a real phenomenon that has theoretically important consequences for the nomination and election of our representatives. Nevertheless, one should not exaggerate the extent to which partisans have become more distinct, as did a Pew Research Center report in late 2003. Provocatively titled *The 2004 Political Landscape: Evenly Divided and Increasingly Polarized,* the study received widespread notice in the media.[12] On the whole the report was excellent, a highly informative summary of extensive surveys conducted between 1987 and 2003. But despite the claim embodied in the title, one strains to find evidence consistent with increasing polarization in the body of the report or in the myriad tables and figures that accompany the text. For example, the report's first page carries the chart depicted in Figure 4.2 purporting to show a country that is "further apart than ever in its political values." Provided that "country" is limited to Democratic and Republican partisans and "ever" means sixteen years, the claim is not exactly false: Democrats and Republicans on average have grown 5 percentage points further apart in twenty-four political and policy attitudes and 4 percentage points further apart in seventeen social and personal attitudes between 1987 and 2003. But despite these increases the absolute differences between Democrats

11 Levendusky, "Sorting in the U.S. Mass Electorate." Thomas M. Carsey and Geoffrey Layman, "Party Polarization and Party Structuring of Policy Attitudes: A Comparison of Three NES Panel Studies." *Political Behavior* 24 (2002): 199–236; Geoffrey Layman and Thomas Carsey, "Party Polarization and 'Conflict Extension' in the American Electorate," *American Journal of Political Science* 46 (2002): 786–802.
12 people-press.org/reports/display.php3?ReportID=196.

FIGURE 4.2
Republicans and Democrats Are Further Apart than Ever

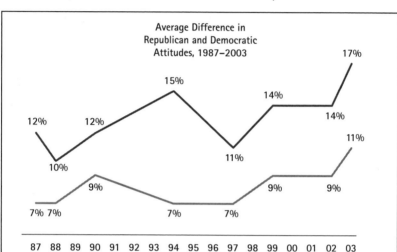

Source: The Pew Research Center for the People & the Press.

and Republicans are relatively small, consistent with those that have been showing up throughout our survey of the evidence. The scale of the Pew figure makes partisan differences look larger than they are, however. In principle, Democratic and Republican differences could range between 0 percent and 100 percent, but as the redrawn plot of the Pew data in Figure 4.3 clearly shows, the partisan disagreement actually observed is only a small fraction of that which could be observed. Rather than "further apart than ever," Figure 4.3 suggests the far less newsworthy conclusion "still close together but maybe not quite as close as in 1987."

Disaggregation of the Pew scales into their more specific components similarly fails to support the title and introduction of the

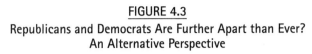

FIGURE 4.3
Republicans and Democrats Are Further Apart than Ever?
An Alternative Perspective

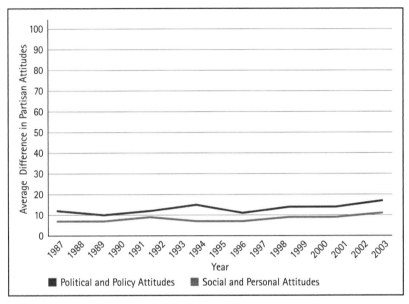

Source: The Pew Research Center for the People & the Press.

report. For example, two pages after making the claim that Americans are "further apart than ever," the report notes that *"Over the past decade there has been a decided shift across the political spectrum in favor of tolerance on issues relating to homosexuality and race"* (p. 3). And later in the report Pew elaborates on those conclusions: *"Since 1987, Americans—both black and white—have become much more personally tolerant. The idea of blacks and whites dating, once highly divisive, is now broadly accepted. There also has been a steady decline in the number of Americans who say they have little in common with people of other races"* (p. 45). Regarding social issues—the heart of the culture wars,

Pew reports that *"Over the past sixteen years, public values on most social issues have remained generally stable . . . . Yet in that period there also has been a distinct shift toward acceptance of several social changes, some of which challenge traditional views of the family"* (p. 69).

In sum, a disinterested reader who digests the 150+ page report comes away with an impression rather different from the harried columnist or reporter who reads only the first page.[13] Rather than indicating "further apart than ever," small increases in the size of opinion differences are intermixed with small decreases and numerous fluctuations without any real pattern. Pew is a highly professional organization with an excellent reputation. Thus, the spin they put on their findings attests to the strength and pervasiveness of the prevailing media frame of a polarized nation.[14]

To continue with the argument advanced in Chapter 2, the inaccurate picture of national polarization presented by the media undoubtedly reflects the fact that the thin stratum of elected officials, political professionals, and party and issue activists who talk to the media are better sorted now than a generation ago. They are more distinct, more ideological, and more polarized than their predecessors. To a lesser extent sorting has made the strongest identifiers in each party more distinct from those of a generation ago. But the polarization story is much less accurate for the less

---

[13] On a *NewsHour with Jim Lehrer* segment entitled "Divided Nation," former Representative Mickey Edwards commented, "But this poll shows a great deal of division among just registered voters, who are not partisans, not activists. . . ." Although that is a defensible rendering of the title and first page of the report, the accompanying data showed no such thing. people-press.org/commentary/display.php3?AnalysisID=73.
[14] Pew would have done better to give its report the subtitle of an earlier report: "An Ambivalent Majority."

strongly identified, let alone for political independents and in general for the mass of citizens who rarely are considered worthy of attention from the media, a point that will be strikingly illustrated in the next chapter when we closely examine the abortion issue.

The following three figures illustrate the general pattern. Figure 4.4 depicts the difference in ideological polarization between the 5–10 percent of the citizenry who are party activists, the 25–30 percent who are strong party identifiers, the 35–40 percent who are only weakly identified, and the 25 percent who profess

FIGURE 4.4
Partisan Polarization on the Liberal–Conservative Scale
Has Increased Slightly over the Past Generation

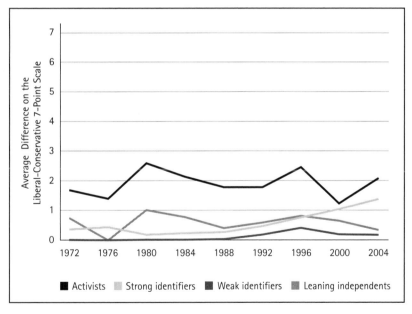

Source: Calculated from the National Election Studies. Activists are defined as party identifiers who report engaging in three or more (of five possible) campaign activities. Party ID measures do not include activists.

independence but admit to leaning toward a party.[15] The activists are several times more polarized than everyone else, but they are not six units apart on the 7-point liberal-conservative scale, they are between two and three units apart.[16] The strongest party identifiers have become somewhat more polarized but they are not six units apart, just one. Weak party identifiers have polarized even less, and independents who lean to a party show no trend at all.

One colleague suggested that "affective" measures might show more evidence of increasing polarization than "cognitive" measures: Republicans and Democrats may be little farther apart on the issues than a generation ago, but they may hate each other much more.[17] The NES includes a measure called the "feeling thermometer" which invites respondents to rate individuals and political groupings on a "very cold" to "very warm" scale. If we compare the difference between ratings of one's own party and ratings of the opposing party (Figure 4.5) we find that there has been little increase in affective polarization since 1980. Strong partisans are far more polarized than weak partisans and independents who lean toward a party, but there is only a slight increase (5–10 degrees) in emotional polarization during the past two decades.[18]

If we compare thermometer ratings of liberals and conservatives (Figure 4.6) we find somewhat more evidence of increasing

---

[15] The remaining 10 percent of Americans deny any leaning toward either party.
[16] The apparent decline in activist polarization in 2000 is presumably sampling error. Only half of the 2000 NES sample was asked the traditional 7-point scale which resulted in only thirty-three Democrats being classified as activists. For some reason they were more moderate than usual.
[17] Sam Popkin deserves the credit or blame for this suggestion.
[18] Interestingly, activists are not quite as favorable to their party and hostile to the other as strong partisans. We have no explanation for this slight difference.

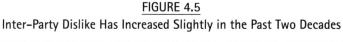

FIGURE 4.5
Inter-Party Dislike Has Increased Slightly in the Past Two Decades

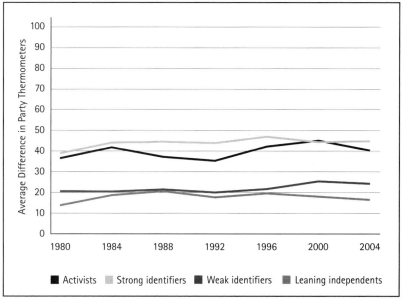

Source: Calculated from the National Election Studies. Activists are defined as party identifiers who report engaging in three or more (of five possible) campaign activities. Party ID measures do not include activists.

emotional polarization—Democratic activists and strong partisans like generic liberals and dislike generic conservatives more than a generation ago, and Republican activists and strong partisans feel just the opposite, but we see the same general pattern of polarization at the top which fades out as partisan commitment declines.[19]

---

[19] See also Evans, "Have Americans' Attitudes Become More Polarized?" Alan Abramowitz and Kyle Saunders, "Ideological Realignment in the U.S. Electorate," *Journal of Politics* 60 (1998): 634–652.

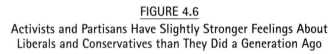

FIGURE 4.6

Activists and Partisans Have Slightly Stronger Feelings About
Liberals and Conservatives than They Did a Generation Ago

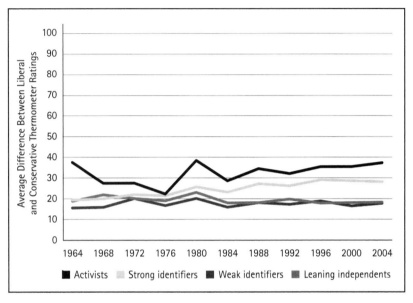

Source: Calculated from the National Election Studies. Activists are defined as party identifiers who
report engaging in three or more (of five possible) campaign activities. Party ID measures do not
include activists.

IS THE COUNTRY POLARIZED?
INDIVIDUALS

A final objection to our consideration of the relative lack of
polarization in the policy preferences of Americans might run
something like this: Okay, so mass attitudes on political issues are
distributed more evenly across states, regions, religions, genders,
ages, races, and even parties and ideologies than popular discussions might have led us to believe, but it still may be the case that

individual voters are more polarized today than they were a generation ago. The red/blue categorization of the journalists and the classic demographic categories of the social scientists simply may not correlate as highly with policy attitudes today because the natural communities of the past have eroded under the assaults of increased geographic mobility and the revolution in communications technology. Citizens now choose their beliefs with less regard to where they live and who they are than in past decades, but individuals are more polarized, nevertheless.

This is a more difficult objection to consider than simply categorizing people in different ways and comparing their similarities and differences, but an earlier research project of ours permits a partial response to the objection. In an analysis that sought to explain Al Gore's surprisingly poor showing in 2000 (relative to standard political science predictive models) we estimated vote choice models for all voters in the elections between 1972 and 2000.[20] The data were drawn from the National Election Studies, and the estimated models incorporated identical survey items asked in each of the eight presidential studies conducted during the period. Vote predictors included party affiliation, ideological self-classification, presidential performance judgments, evaluations of the two major candidates, and evaluations of economic conditions in the country. The statistical output of the estimated equations consists of probabilities that the voter would support the Republican or Democratic candidate.[21]

---

[20] Morris Fiorina, Samuel Abrams, and Jeremy Pope, "The 2000 US Presidential Election: Can Retrospective Voting Be Saved?" *British Journal of Political Science* 33 (2003): 163–187.
[21] The estimation method was probit analysis. It generates predicted probabilities of voting for Bush versus Gore, which are the basis of the figure.

Now, although this analysis focuses on voters' *choices*, not their *positions*, if individual voter positions have become more polarized over time, then other things being equal, we might expect to see an increase in the number of voters predicted to vote for one candidate with very high probability and the other candidate with very low probability, or equivalently, a decrease in voters with probabilities of voting for the two candidates that are close to 50:50. Since there is no generally agreed-upon definition of what is very high probability, we present the results for three increasingly strict definitions: 70:30, 80:20, and 90:10. As shown in Figure 4.7 the exact definition of polarization makes little difference. Taking

FIGURE 4.7
Levels of Individual Voter Polarization

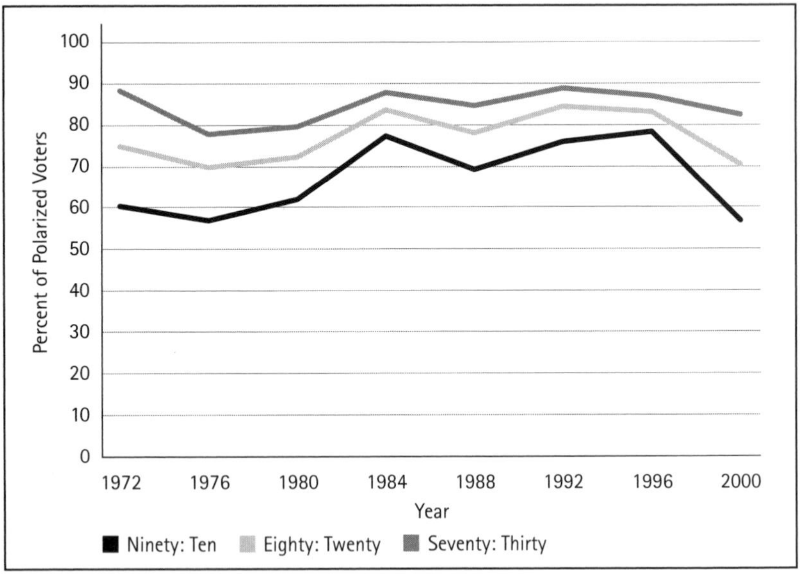

Source: Calculated from the National Election Studies.

a strict definition of polarization (90:10) we see that about 60 percent of the electorate was polarized in the 1972–1980 elections, a figure that increased 10–15 percent in the Reagan–Clinton years, but then *declined* in 2000. The same pattern holds with less strict definitions of polarization—a rise in the Reagan–Clinton years, but a drop in 2000. On the whole the estimated levels of individual vote polarization are relatively high overall, but polarization in 2000 was about the same as in the Ford–Carter election of 1976. Like the 2000 election, that was a very close election, but in contrast to the commentary surrounding 2000, we do not recall much talk of how polarized the country was in 1976.

IS THE COUNTRY POLARIZED?
ADDITIONAL PERSPECTIVES

Since publication of the first edition of this book other scholars have published significant works that help to correct the prevailing distorted image of politics in America. Their data and methods differ from ours, but their conclusions do not: reports of an increasingly polarized America are greatly exaggerated.

One claim that got considerable press during the 2004 campaign was that increasing geographical segregation was reinforcing the political differences among Americans, not just at the gross level of red-blue states, but at the finer county level that better reflects the day-to-day context in which Americans live and work.[22] Some commentators jumped to the conclusion that

---

[22] Bill Bishop, "The Schism in U.S. Politics Begins at Home," *Austin American-Statesman*, April 4, 2004; Bill Bishop," The Cost of Political Uniformity," *Austin American-Statesman*, April 8, 2004; Bill Bishop,"Poltics 2004: Preach to the Choir," *Austin American-Statesman*, May 2, 2004. (www .statesman.com/specialreports/content/specialreports/greatdivide/index.html).

Americans increasingly were living their lives in culturally and politically homogeneous neighborhoods where majority-held opinions would be reinforced and minority-held opinions suppressed. On the contrary, Klinkner showed that in 2000 fewer Americans lived in electorally homogeneous counties than in five of the twelve presidential elections between 1952 and 1996, most recently that of 1988.[23] Moreover, the distribution of the 2000 presidential vote across all 3000 or so American counties was not bimodal—with large numbers of heavily Gore and heavily Bush counties, but unimodal with most counties falling in the central, competitive range. A 2004 update of the analysis shows a similar lack of geographical polarization.[24]

Counties are still rather heterogeneous units, of course, so a further useful addition to the discussion is a study conducted by the Brookings Institution which reported that in the nation's ten largest metropolitan areas racial and ethnic integration of neighborhoods *increased* significantly during the 1990s.[25] Predominantly white neighborhoods fell by 30 percent during the decade, with integration occurring not only in blue state cities but in red state ones like Atlanta, Dallas, and Houston. Given the strong correlation between racial and ethnic minority status and partisan voting, this evidence suggests that more urban residents, at least, were living in politically heterogeneous neighborhoods in 2000 than in 1990.

---

23 Philip Klinkner, "Red and Blue Scare: The Continuing Diversity of the American Electoral Landscape," *The Forum*: 2 (2004). www.bepress.co/forum.
24 Philip A. Klinkner and Ann Hapanowicz, "Red and Blue Déjà Vu: Measuring Political Polarization in the 2004 Election," *The Forum*: 3 (2005). www.bepress.com/forum/vol3/iss2/art2.
25 David Fasenfest, Jason Booza, and Kurt Metzger, "Living Together: A New Look at Racial and Ethnic Integration in Metropolitan Neighborhoods, 1990–2000." www.brookings.edu/metro/publications/20040428_fasenfest.htm.

Finally, Baker's major work, *America's Crisis of Values* includes a chapter entitled "Culture War."[26] His analysis utilizes data from the World Values Surveys conducted between 1981 and 2000. Interestingly, Baker reports support for James Davison Hunter's contention that Americans show some increased polarization at the level of moral visions—"absolutists" versus "relativists," mainly because the number of absolutists rose between 1980 and 1990. But contrary to what is assumed by some commentators, the abstract moral visions of Americans do not have much relation to their values or their political positions. Most Americans hold both traditional values but also hold more modern self-expressive values, and both affect their political positions. Baker concludes:

> *Almost all social attitudes—even about emotionally charged issues such as homosexuality—are not polarized. Moreover, most social attitudes are converging, becoming even more similar over time. The notable exception is attitudes about abortion. Religious values are not polarized. Most Americans are religious centrists, located between the extremes of religious orthodoxy and moral progressivism. Cultural values are not polarized. Most Americans cluster toward the traditional pole of the traditional/secular-rational dimension. There is some evidence of the polarization of moral visions, but this is a tendency, not the basis of two morally opposed camps, because absolutists and relativists still have a lot in common.[27]*

In sum, Americans who believe in a transcendent God and a fixed moral code are not automatically cultural conservatives, and

---

[26] Wayne Baker, *America's Crisis of Values* (Princeton NJ: Princeton University Press, 2003).
[27] Ibid., 103–4.

those who have a more relativistic view are not automatically cultural liberals.

SUMMARY: NOT A POLARIZED ELECTORATE

To some degree, polarization is a subjective judgment. For some people a 10 percent difference in the preferences of a state or a socioeconomic group on abortion or gay rights may be sufficient to conclude that the American electorate is engaged in a culture war. Our judgment differs. Granted, in a majority rule electoral system 10 percentage point differences that occur in the neighborhood of 50 percent may be politically very consequential. A jurisdiction with a small right-of-center majority may elect a hard-right Republican representative while another with a small left-of-center majority may elect a hard-left Democrat. But to infer from the polarization of the election winners that voters in the first jurisdiction overwhelmingly disagree with voters in the second jurisdiction is both a logical error and a conclusion at odds with the data.

On the contrary, the data presented in this and the preceding chapter indicate that while Republican and Democratic partisans are better sorted today than several decades ago, reports of an American population polarized around moral and religious issues—or any other issue for that matter—are greatly exaggerated. That is especially true for the red/blue state categorization so popular in the contemporary media, but it is true as well when one looks at traditional demographic categories dear to the hearts of sociologists and political scientists. Even taking the analysis down to the level of individual voters reveals that while a majority of

Americans go to the polls with a fairly set idea of how they will cast their votes, that majority was no bigger in 2000 than in 1976. Reports of a culture war are mostly wishful thinking and useful fund-raising strategies on the part of culture war guerrillas, abetted by a media driven by the need to make the dull and everyday appear exciting and unprecedented.

In one of its articles on the 50:50 nation the *Economist* remarked in passing that a misprint in one draft had rendered the phrase, the "so-so nation."[28] Unintentional though it was, that misprint better describes the state of American public opinion than do the commentaries of many political pundits.

---

[28] "On his high horse," *The Economist*, November 9, 2002: 25.

FIGURE 4.1
Polarization vs. Sorting

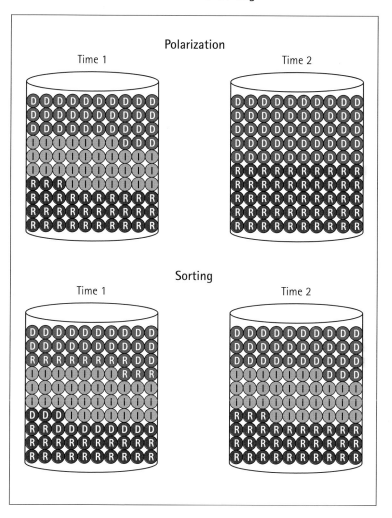

CHAPTER 5

A Closer Look at Abortion

In 1973 the Supreme Court decided *Roe v. Wade*, striking down any restrictions on a woman's right to terminate a pregnancy in the first trimester and limiting restrictions on that right in the second trimester. In the ensuing three decades abortion has remained on the national agenda, and many observers came to regard it as the defining issue in the culture wars. Luker describes how the right-to-life movement grew in reaction to the *Roe* decision.[1] And, more broadly, there is little doubt that antiabortion activism was an important component of the development of the religious right in the 1970s. The religious right, of course, defines the "orthodox" position in the purported culture wars.

For a subject that has been so much studied and discussed there are a surprising number of major misconceptions about public attitudes toward abortion. Indeed, to a considerable extent the general

---

[1] Kristin Luker, *Abortion and the Politics of Motherhood* (Berkeley, CA: University of California Press, 1984).

myth of a culture war probably rests on several more specific myths about public opinion on abortion. For example, we are often told that the country is polarized on the issue of abortion. This claim is false. Similarly, we often hear the related claim that abortion is an issue that is not susceptible to compromise. This claim too is false—at least from the standpoint of the great majority of Americans. Finally, we often hear and read that because of the parties' stands on abortion a gender gap has developed, wherein women disproportionately support the pro-choice Democratic Party while men disproportionately support the pro-life Republican Party. Again, this claim is false: the gender gap is real, to be sure, but contrary to popular commentary, it has little or nothing to do with abortion. We hasten to add that we are not telling disinterested analysts of public opinion anything new here, but there is a large gap between what academic analysts know to be fact and what political debate and media commentary depict as fact.[2]

PUBLIC ATTITUDES TOWARD ABORTION: "I'M 'PRO-CHOICE,' BUT . . ."

As with most topics in public opinion polling, question wording makes a great deal of difference in how people respond to questions about abortion, a fact that both the pro-choice and pro-life sides of the debate naturally exploit. The antiabortion side emphasizes the act of aborting a potential life. Polls consistently show that many Americans are troubled by abortion; indeed, as

---

[2] For an excellent earlier survey of public opinion on abortion see Elizabeth Cook, Ted Jelen, and Clyde Wilcox, *Between Two Absolutes* (Boulder, CO: Westview Press, 1992).

TABLE 5.1
Is Abortion Murder?

"Some people say that abortion is an act of murder, while other people disagree with this. What is your view—do you think that abortion is an act of murder or don't you feel this way?"

	ACT OF MURDER	DON'T FEEL THIS WAY
January 1995	40%	51%
January 1998	48	45
January 2003	46	46

Source: Everett Ladd and Karlyn Bowman, *Public Opinion About Abortion*, Washington, DC: AEI Press, 2nd ed. 2000: 26. The 2003 figures were supplied by Karlyn Bowman. The original data are taken from surveys using identical question wording by Yankelovich, Gallup, and Harris/CNN/Time, respectively.

Table 5.1 shows, about as many respondents in national surveys opine that abortion is murder as deny that it is.[3] But—and this is a critically important point—not everyone who believes that abortion is wrong—not even everyone who believes it is murderous—supports making it illegal. For, just as consistently, over the past fifteen years national polls report that a majority of Americans believe in the principle of choice, and support for *Roe* now approaches the two-thirds majority level (Figure 5.1).[4] The juxtaposition of these two findings logically implies that a significant number of people who believe that abortion is wrong nevertheless support the principle of a woman's right to choose as embodied in *Roe*.

---

[3] Surveys by other polling organizations using slightly different question wordings report very similar findings. See Grew Shaw, "Poll Trends: Abortion," *Public Opinion Quarterly* 67 (2003): 415.

[4] Other polling organizations sometimes report lower support for *Roe* than does Gallup, but almost invariably they report a comfortable majority of Americans in support. Ibid: 426.

FIGURE 5.1

A Clear Majority of Americans Now Supports *Roe v. Wade*

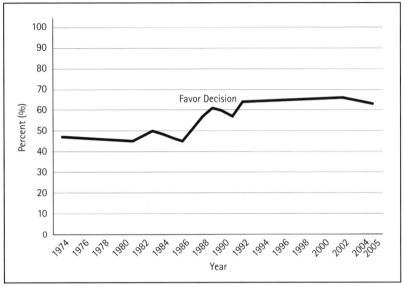

Source: The Gallup Poll.

There is no necessary logical inconsistency here, of course; many people may simply decline to impose their personal views on the rest of society. Nor does the juxtaposition of pro-choice with antiabortion attitudes mean that Americans are confused or uncertain about abortion as they are about some complex technical issues. As noted, abortion has been on the agenda for some three decades and there is reason to believe that most Americans long ago decided where they stood on the issue. When the *same* survey question is repeated over time, public opinion is strikingly stable. The General Social Survey has included the following item for three decades:

Please tell me whether or not you think it should be possible for a pregnant woman to obtain a legal abortion if

1. *the woman's own health is seriously endangered.*
2. *she became pregnant as a result of rape.*
3. *there is a strong chance of serious defect in the baby.*
4. *the family has very low income and cannot afford any more children.*
5. *she is not married and does not want to marry the man.*
6. *she is married and does not want any more children.*

This item omits any reference to the emotionally charged rhetoric of the abortion debate and focuses purely on the substance of people's beliefs. Figure 5.2 shows that after moving in a liberal direction in the early 1970s, opinion stabilized at the time of the *Roe* decision, stayed remarkably constant for two decades, and then moved a bit in a conservative direction in the late 1990s.[5] On average, Americans favor legal abortion in slightly less than four of the six circumstances, with huge majorities supporting abortion in the first three ("traumatic") circumstances, but bare majorities or only minorities supporting abortion in the second three ("elective") circumstances.[6] Opinion appears to have changed little after the 1989 *Webster* decision, which opened the way for further state regulation of abortion, and after the 1992 *Casey* decision,

---

[5] As in Figure 5.2, numerous surveys registered a slight downturn in support for legal abortion in the late 1990s. In recent years some pro-life groups have focused attention on an abortion procedure called "intact dilation and extraction" or "partial birth abortion," in which the fetus is destroyed after it has been partially delivered. Pictures and verbal descriptions offered by pro-life groups are quite gruesome, and large majorities of Americans have consistently registered opposition to this particular procedure. Thus, the debate probably sensitized some generally pro-choice Americans to the fact that they have conditional views on the issue, leading to a drop in unqualified support.

[6] The terms "traumatic" and "elective" are those commonly used by researchers in the area and are not used here in any evaluative sense.

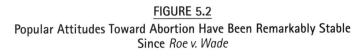

FIGURE 5.2

Popular Attitudes Toward Abortion Have Been Remarkably Stable
Since *Roe v. Wade*

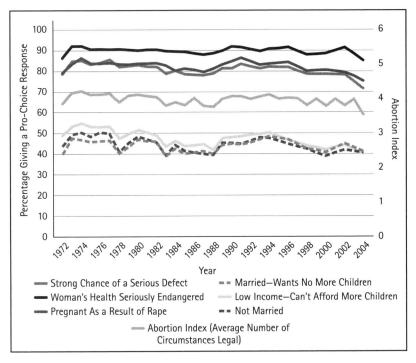

Source: Calculated from the General Social Surveys.

which upheld some of the specific restrictions imposed by the state
of Pennsylvania.

As we would expect, attitudes toward abortion vary across the
regions of the country, but the differences are smaller than political commentary would lead most readers to expect. As Figure 5.3
shows, in 2000, residents of the red states supported legal abortion in about 3.5 of the six circumstances, a bit lower than the
national average, while residents of the blue states supported

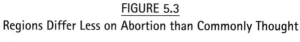

FIGURE 5.3

Regions Differ Less on Abortion than Commonly Thought

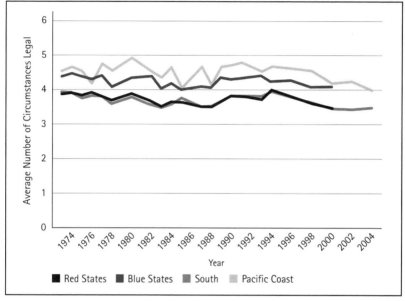

Source: Calculated from the General Social Surveys.
Note: State level data for 2002 and 2004 not yet available.

abortion in about 4 circumstances, a little higher than the national average. As we noted in the preceding chapter, however, states are gross units of analysis. In particular, the blue states of the northeast and Great Lakes have a heavy Catholic presence and are home to many socially conservative Democrats. But even if we refine the categories and compare the deep red states of the old confederacy with the blue states of the Pacific Coast, even in 2004 we see surprisingly small differences: citizens of the libertine "left coast" indeed are on average more pro-choice than citizens of the traditionally minded southern states, but the difference is not zero

versus six circumstances, but rather 3.5 versus 4. Regional differences are marginal, not major.

Just as regional differences on abortion are smaller than often
assumed, so are religious differences. Indeed, Jews are the only
group that differs markedly from the national average—most favor
legal abortion in all circumstances. As Figure 5.4 shows, however,
Evangelical Protestants differ from mainline Protestants by less
than one circumstance out of six, and the average Catholic falls
between the two Protestant categories, supporting legal abortion in
about 3.5 of the six circumstances. Given that the clergy of the
Catholic and Evangelical churches are commonly portrayed as

FIGURE 5.4
Religious Denominations Differ Less on Abortion than Stereotypes Suggest

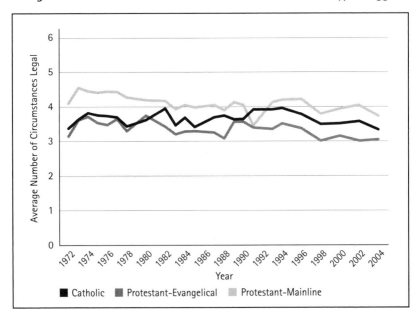

Source: Calculated from the General Social Surveys.

leaders in the right-to-life camp, it is surprising that their rank-and-file express opinions so similar to the rest of the population.

As we will discuss in Chapter 7, in today's world denomination often is less important than religiosity, or a person's degree of religious commitment; hence, Figure 5.4 may understate the connection between religion and abortion attitudes. Figure 5.5 plots support for legal abortion as a function of a measure of religious commitment—church attendance—perhaps more revealing than denomination. Again, the figures tend in the expected direction:

FIGURE 5.5
The Churched and the Unchurched Differ Less on Abortion than Stereotypes Suggest

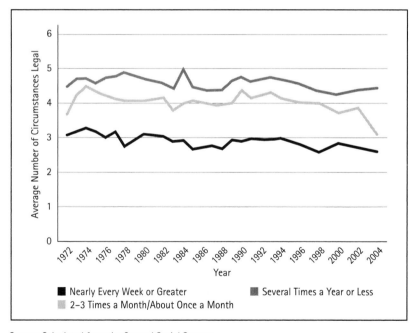

Source: Calculated from the General Social Surveys.

nonchurchgoers are more pro-choice than the national average, while regular churchgoers are almost a full circumstance below the national average. But, again, the difference between these categories is not six circumstances on the index, or even three or four, but about two circumstances—not exactly a religious war.

No doubt Figure 5.6 will surprise many people. The contemporary Democrats indisputably are the pro-choice party. Democratic presidential candidates must pass a litmus test, and the party even refused to allow the pro-life governor of an electorally

FIGURE 5.6
Partisans in the General Public Do Not Differ Much on Abortion

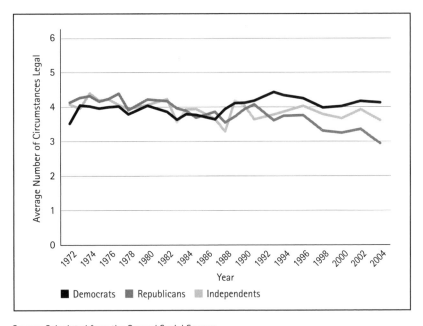

Source: Calculated from the General Social Surveys.
Note: Partisans include strong and weak identifiers.

important state to speak at the 1996 convention.[7] Just as indisputably the contemporary Republicans are the pro-life party. Republican presidential candidates must pass a litmus test that is the opposite of the Democrats'.[8] Apparently, the word has only recently gotten out to most of the party rank-and-file, however. As previous analysts have noted, when *Roe* was decided and for some years thereafter, Republicans were ever so slightly more pro-choice than Democrats. Reflecting the partisan sorting we discussed in Chapter 4, only since the early 1990s have self-identified Democrats in the population been consistently more pro-choice than self-identified Republicans, and the difference did not reach a full unit on the six-circumstance index until 2004. Given the strong association between the parties' activists and candidates with opposing sides of the abortion issue, the weak differentiation of partisans at the mass level is noteworthy.[9]

Because Figure 5.6 is so counter to much of the conventional wisdom it is worthwhile to show that it is not an artifact of the NORC survey question. Figure 5.7 plots the responses of Democrats and Republicans to a very different Gallup survey item that asks simply, "Do you think abortion should be legal under any circumstances, legal only under certain circumstances, or illegal in all

---

[7] Robert Casey of Pennsylvania. Richard Gephardt, a pro-life Missouri Baptist, had a pro-choice epiphany before deciding to seek the 1988 Democratic presidential nomination, as did Dennis Kucinich, a pro-life Ohio Catholic before entering the 2004 race for the nomination. Al Gore's conversion (he denies there was one) took place less suddenly. See Walter Robinson and Ann Scales, "Campaign 2000: Gore Record Scrutinized for Veracity," *Boston Globe*, January 28, 2000: A1.

[8] In 1980 George H. W. Bush was a tolerant New England Episcopalian. By 1988 he was a born-again social conservative. In 1996 plutocrat Steve Forbes was an economic conservative with little interest in social and cultural issues. By the time he again sought the nomination in 2000 he was a committed social conservative.

[9] In Figure 5.6, as elsewhere in this book, strong and weak identifiers are classified as partisans. If independents who lean toward a party are classified as partisans—a coding practice that some political scientists prefer, partisan differences all but disappear.

FIGURE 5.7
When Should Abortion be Legal? Partisans Are Not Very Different

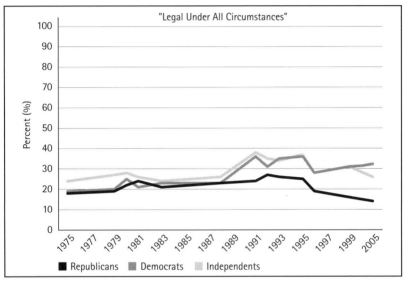

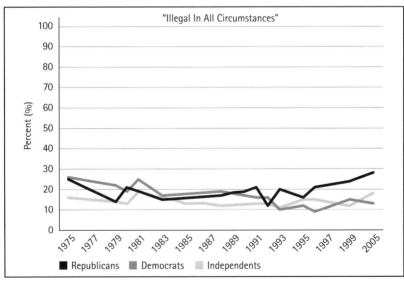

Source: The Gallup Organization.

circumstances?" A majority of Americans consistently responds "legal only under certain circumstances." Consider the partisan gap in the two more extreme responses chosen by minorities of the population. Beginning in the early 1990s (in response to *Webster?*) a partisan gap of 10 to 15 points opened up at the liberal extreme. Democrats are 10 to 15 points more likely than Republicans to say "legal under any circumstances," but note that only 30–35 percent of Democrats choose that response. In turn, Republicans are about 10 to 15 points more likely to say "illegal in all circumstances," but only 20–25 percent of Republicans take that position. Depending on the year a little more than 50 percent of Republicans and a little less than 50 percent of Democrats choose "legal only under certain circumstances."

The preceding figures tell a story about American abortion attitudes that differs greatly from that told by political and media commentators for three decades. We hear repeatedly that the Republicans are culturally "orthodox," the party of the right-to-life movement in particular and the religious right in general. The Democrats are culturally "progressive," the party of the right-to-choose movement in particular and secular humanism in general. Such generalizations have a good deal of validity when describing the parties' officeholders, activists, and associated cause groups, but they are gross exaggerations of differences between the parties' adherents within the broader public.

To be sure, the lack of association between citizens' party affiliations and their views on abortion does not prove that the *labels* "pro-life" and "pro-choice" may have taken on broader connotations, something on the order of "intolerant puritans" on the one hand versus "degenerate libertines" on the other. Thus, voters may be more divided over the labels "pro-life" and "pro-choice" than over actual policy alternatives.[10] But whatever the connotations the labels have taken on, the evidence is clear that the broad American public is not polarized on the specifics of the abortion issue. They believe that abortion should be legal but that it is reasonable to regulate it in various ways. They are "pro-choice, buts." Recognizing this state of public opinion, Bill Clinton, one of the most adroit politicians of our era, said that he was pro-choice and against abortion, and we think that Americans understood exactly what he meant. To the chagrin of some of the absolutist pro-choice groups in the Democratic base, prospective 2008 presidential candidate Senator Hillary Clinton has staked out a similar position.[11]

Americans are traditionally pragmatic, and they approach even an issue like abortion in a pragmatic fashion. They favor the right to choose, but only a small minority favors the right to choose in every conceivable circumstance.[12] Overwhelming majorities

---

10 Just as women were more favorable toward government efforts to improve the status of women than they were toward the term "feminist." See "What Women Think about the Feminist Label," *Public Perspective*, November/December 1991: 92–93.

11 In January 2005 in a speech marking the anniversary of *Roe v. Wade*, Senator Hillary Clinton made headlines by advocating a change in the Democratic Party's stance on the abortion issue. A careful reading of her remarks showed that she was appealing to the sentiments held by the vast majority of Americans who are not completely committed to either side of the debate. David Garrow, "Pro-Choice groups giving up too much?" www.csmonitor.com, February 23, 2005.

12 Moreover, polls probably overestimate the size of the unconditionally pro-choice minority. Bartels reports that in the 1996 NES study about 40 percent reported that they believed a woman should "always be able" to obtain a legal abortion, but when re-interviewed the next year, about 40 percent of those same unconditionally pro-choice respondents favored a ban on partial birth abortions and another 12 percent of them were undecided. See Larry Bartels, "Is 'Popular Rule' Possible?" *Brookings Review* 21 (2003): 14. Along similar lines, a September 2004 YouGov Internet survey on which one of us consulted included the GSS abortion battery plus one additional circumstance: gender selection. While 31 percent of the sample thought abortion should be legal if "the woman wants it for any reason," one-third of those people thought abortion to select the sex of the baby should not be legal. It appears that many people who unreflectively answer "always" or "under any circumstances" don't really believe that when probed. Probably the same is true for Americans who claim they are unconditionally pro-life, but we have no data to test this supposition.

regard rape, birth defects, and threats to the mother's life and health as sufficient justifications for abortion, while clear majorities regard personal convenience and gender selection as insufficient. Opinion divides on justifications based on the mother's age, financial condition, and marital status. In this light it was not surprising that at the same time that a two-thirds majority of Americans endorsed *Roe*, about 60 percent of the public also endorsed *Casey* (and Democrats were just as supportive as Republicans), approved of state laws that made abortion more difficult, and opposed public funding of abortion (Tables 5.2 and 5.3). Political folklore holds that the Supreme Court follows the election returns, but in the abortion decisions, it can fairly be said that the Supreme Court followed public opinion, as Justice Scalia complained in his dissent in *Casey*.[13]

In sum, public opinion on abortion does not support militants on either side of the issue. Militants think in terms of unconditional rights. Pro-choice activists who play an important role in the Democratic Party argue that any infringement on a woman's right to choose is unacceptable, even if that means the occasional abortion of a healthy, near-term fetus. Such people probably comprise less than 10 percent of the population. Pro-life activists who play an important role in the Republican Party argue that any abortion is unacceptable, even if that means the occasional death of a woman. Such people certainly comprise less than 10 percent of the population. The great majority of the American citizenry rejects extreme positions and would accept compromise laws, but

---

13 *Planned Parenthood of Southeastern Pa. v. Casey* (91-744), 505 U.S. 833 (1992).

TABLE 5.2
Abortion: Post-Casey

As you may know, the Supreme Court recently decided that a woman still has the right to have an abortion until the fetus is viable, but said that certain restrictions—such as a twenty-four hour waiting period, parental consent for girls under eighteen, and requiring doctors to provide information on alternatives to abortion—are legal as long as an undue burden is not placed on a woman seeking an abortion. In general, do you approve or disapprove of the Supreme Court's decision?

	APPROVING
National	59%
Republicans	58
Democrats	58
Independents	62

Source: *American Viewpoint*, July 8–13, 1992.

TABLE 5.3
Abortion: In Some Circumstances

	OPPOSE	FAVOR
Would you like to see *Roe v. Wade* overturned? (after explanation)	65%	35%
Would you support or oppose the following legislative restrictions (except in threat to mother's life)?		
Counseling on dangers and alternatives	9	91
Parental permission	23	77
No public funding	36	64
Fetal viability testing	38	62
No public facilities	33	57
No public employees	56	44

Source: Gallup, July 6–7, 1989.

such compromises are hard to achieve given the polarization of the political class.[14]

ABORTION AND THE GENDER GAP

Yet another staple of contemporary political commentary is the gender gap in support for the major parties beginning with Ronald Reagan's defeat of Jimmy Carter in 1980. In presidential elections (Figure 5.8) and increasingly in congressional elections, women have voted consistently more Democratic than men, a trend that reached its height—so far—in the 1996 election when the gap between men's and women's support for Bill Clinton reached double digits—almost 15 points. (Several polls suggested that Robert Dole would have narrowly won the election had only men voted).[15] Pro-choice groups have seized on the gender gap to argue that Republicans are out of step with American women on the issue of abortion, a charge uncritically echoed by politicians and pundits:

Democrats believe women will reject Bush because of his conservative positions on issues such as abortion.[16]

---

[14] Arguably the difficulty of compromising has been greater for the Republicans, many of whose activists are committed to changing a status quo that a majority of the country accepts. See David Brady and Edward Schwartz, "Abortion Politics in the U.S. Senate," *Public Choice* 84 (1995): 25–48. More recently the controversy over partial birth abortion has created greater difficulties for the Democrats. Note that in Europe, where citizen activists and interest groups are less influential relative to party professionals, compromise abortion laws have been much less difficult to adopt than in the United States.

[15] Note that the gender gap closed up significantly in 2004. The 5 percent lower women's vote for Kerry in 2004 relative to Gore in 2000 covers the popular vote margin by which Bush won in 2004. In Chapter 8 we discuss the diminished gender gap in 2004.

[16] Judy Keen, "Bush Is Working to Woo Female Voters," *USA Today,* March 6, 2000: 10A.

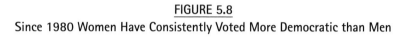

FIGURE 5.8

Since 1980 Women Have Consistently Voted More Democratic than Men

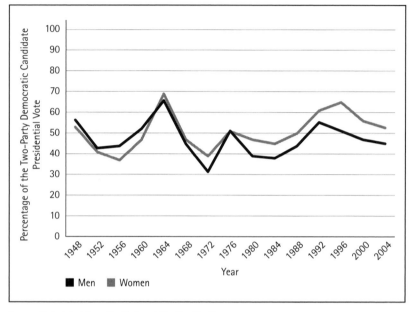

Source: Calculated from the National Election Studies.

In California, the abortion issue holds enormous sway among women who have provided a crucial "gender gap" margin-of-victory vote.[17]

Just as the Christian right created a gender gap by its opposition to abortion, so Dean will trigger a values gap that will send moderate voters flocking in droves to the Republicans.[18]

---

[17] Carla Marinucci, "At S.F. Meeting, Pro-Choice GOP Women Lament Their Bitter Dilemma," *San Francisco Chronicle*, March 11, 2000: A3.

[18] Dick Morris, "McGovern II . . ." *New York Post* online edition, July 9, 2003: 2.

Here is another myth about American politics. Yes, the gender gap is politically significant. So is the abortion issue. Moreover, as we saw in the preceding section, extreme pro-life Republicans *are* out of step with American women on the issue. But they are out of step with men as well, and the same holds for extreme pro-choice Democrats.[19] The simple albeit surprising fact is that the gender gap is not a reflection of differing men's and women's views about abortion: there is no evidence that the abortion issue has anything to do with the gender gap. Claims to the contrary are myth.

Public opinion analysts have long known that men and women do not differ on the subject of abortion, and as in Figure 5.9, whatever small differences appear often reflect the fact that men are slightly more pro-choice than women—for understandable, if crass reasons. This negative finding extends beyond abortion to the full range of explicitly "women's issues." As Jane Mansbridge pointed out after the 1980 elections, men and women do not differ on such issues—contrary to widespread (mis)interpretations in the media and in the political arena, the roots of the gender gap lie elsewhere.[20]

Again, to emphasize that this lack of gender differences transcends the particular survey items used to examine them, we note

---

[19] Even academics sometimes forget their professional training when discussing this issue. For example, John Judis and (political scientist) Ruy Texeira write "But one issue that concerned female voters directly as women and clearly turned many college-educated women toward the Democratic Party was the Republican Party's opposition to abortion." In support they cite women's opinions on the issue but nowhere compare them with those of men. See Judis and Texeira, *The Emerging Democratic Majority* (New York: Scribner, 2002): 54–55.

[20] Jane Mansbridge, "The ERA and the 1980 Elections," *Public Opinion Quarterly* 49 (1985): 164–78. See also Elizabeth Adell Cook and Clyde Wilcox, "Feminism and the Gender Gap—A Second Look," *Journal of Politics* 53 (1991): 1111–1122.

FIGURE 5.9
Men and Women Do Not Differ on Abortion

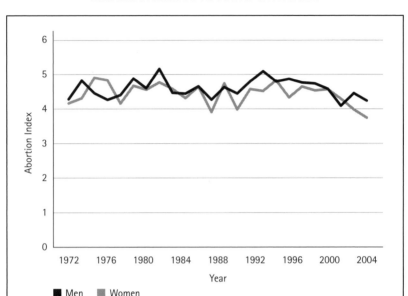

Source: Calculated from the General Social Surveys.

that on the aforementioned Gallup survey item women are five to eight points more likely to favor legal abortion "under all circumstances" than are men, and also a couple of percentage points more likely to think that abortion should be "illegal in all circumstances" than are men. Figure 5.10 illustrates the minimal gender differences on this item.

Of course, one might object that even if men and women do not differ much on abortion, if women considered the issue much more important than men, a gap could still result. While this is an eminently plausible hypothesis that is accepted uncritically by many in the media and in politics, research finds little support for

FIGURE 5.10
When Should Abortion Be Legal? Men and Women Are Not Very Different

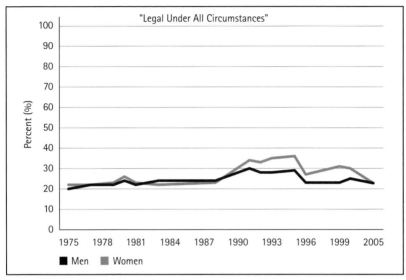

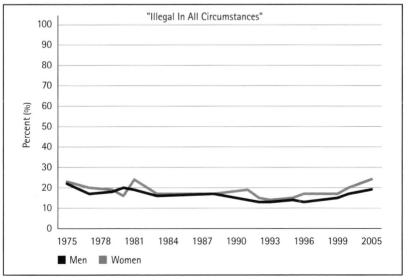

Source: The Gallup Organization.

it. Instead, election studies show no consistent pattern. In 1992 "feminist issues" (including abortion) were more important predictors of women's presidential votes than men's, but in 1996 the reverse was the case.[21] And another study concluded that abortion did not matter for either men or women in 1980, it mattered more for *men* in 1984 and 1988, and mattered for both men and women in 1992, although somewhat more for women.[22]

If the gender gap is not caused by abortion, then from what issues does it arise? Research finds that men's and women's views differ on two clusters of issues, a sampling of which appears in Table 5.4.[23] The first consists of issues of violence, the use of force, and peace and war.[24] For example, women are less likely to support the death penalty, more likely to favor gun control, and less likely to favor going to war. A particularly striking example of this sort of gender gap emerged in 1994, when an American teenager living in Singapore who had vandalized property, was sentenced to a traditional Singaporean punishment of caning. A majority of the mothers and sisters of America considered the sentence barbaric, while a majority of the fathers and brothers viewed it as appropriate—the item produced a 22-point gender gap.

The second cluster of issues on which men and women differ has to do with protecting the vulnerable—the aged, the sick, the poor, and other "at risk" categories. Women are more compas-

---

21 Karen Kaufmann and John Petrocik, "The Changing Politics of American Men: Understanding the Sources of the Gender Gap," *American Journal of Political Science* 43 (1999): 880–81.
22 Carole Chaney, R. Michael Alvarez, and Jonathan Nagler, "Explaining the Gender Gap in U.S. Presidential Elections, 1980–1992, *Political Research Quarterly* 51 (1998): 311–39.
23 Robert Shapiro and Harpreet Mahajan, "Gender Differences in Policy Preferences: A Summary of Trends from the 1960s to the 1980s," *Public Opinion Quarterly* 50 (1986): 42–61.
24 Pamela Johnston Conover and Virginia Sapiro, "Gender, Feminist Constiousness, and War," *American Journal of Political Science* 37 (1993): 1079–99.

TABLE 5.4
Women's and Men's Attitudes Differ

	WOMEN	MEN
Role of Government		
Consider self conservative	29%	43%
Government should provide fewer services	30	45
Poverty and homelessness are among the country's most important problems	63	44
Favor affirmative action programs for blacks and other minority groups	69	58
Force/Violence		
American bombers should attack all military targets in Iraq, including those in heavily populated areas	37	61
Handguns should be illegal except for use by police and other authorized persons	48	28
Favor death penalty	76	82
Approve of caning the teenager in Singapore who committed acts of vandalism	39	61
Approve of the way the Justice Department took Elian Gonzalez from his Miami relatives	35	52

Source: *The Public Perspective*, August/September 1996: 10–27; *The Public Perspective*, July/August 1994: 96. Gallup Tuesday Briefing, May 2, 2000.

sionate, registering higher levels of support for government programs to help the disadvantaged and greater willingness to support government spending for the disadvantaged.[25] Thus, women favor a more activist government than men, and are slightly more likely

---

[25] See Ann Beutal and Margaret Marini," Gender and Values," *American Sociological Review* 60 (1995): 436–48. Vincent Hutchings, Nicholas Valentino, Tasha Philpot, and Ismail White, "The Compassion Strategy: Race and the Gender Gap in Campaign 2000," *Public Opinion Quarterly* 68 (2004): 512–41. Karen Kaufmann, "The Partisan Paradox: Religious Commitment and the Gender Gap in Party Identification," *Public Opinion Quarterly* 68 (2004): 491–511.

to label themselves liberals and less likely to label themselves conservatives.

Why do men and women differ in these ways? This is a matter of spirited debate. Some argue that gender differences are biological, that women and men are hard-wired differently. Others vehemently reject such arguments and attribute gender differences to cultural factors—women and men still are socialized to have different values. Still others contend that gender differences reflect the relatively greater economic vulnerability of women. The gender gap is much larger among single men and women than among married men and women.[26] So, as marriage rates have declined in recent decades the gender gap has grown accordingly.[27] Finally, some argue that the gender gap arises from different experiences and information. Even today women are far more likely to visit the aged and the sick in hospitals, volunteer in the schools, and otherwise see government programs in operation, while men think of government mostly in terms of deductions from their paychecks. Similarly, popular women's magazines and television programs focus on threats to the food supply and the environment and the necessity for mothers to protect their children, while popular men's magazines and television programs focus on sports and women. In contrast to men, women more often see the benefits of government programs as well as the costs.

---

[26] See page 16 of the Pew Report discussed in the preceding chapter. A recent story in *USA Today* claims that married couples—especially educated ones—are increasingly split, but only anecdotes are presented in support. All the systematic data presented refer to men and women without regard to marital status. Susan Page, "Highly Educated Couples Often Split on Candidates," *USA Today*, December 18, 2003: 1A–2A.

[27] Lena Edlund and Rohini Pande, "Why Have Women Become Left-Wing? The Political Gender Gap and the Decline in Marriage," *Quarterly Journal of Economics* 117 (2002): 917–61.

As political scientists we are not professionally qualified to judge among such contending explanations of the gender gap. We can only emphasize that the gender gap in voting has its roots in gender differences on issues other than abortion. The reason that the gender gap has emerged in the past two decades is that the Democratic Party has come to be associated both with an activist government that supports the vulnerable and disadvantaged, and with a more pacifistic foreign and defense policy. In the mid-twentieth century, however, the Republican Party was seen as the party best able to keep the peace. In the 1950s, women voted for Republican Dwight Eisenhower at higher levels than men did. Eisenhower promised to end the war in Korea—and did—and declined to become involved in Vietnam. And as shown in Figure 5.8, women in 1960 voted more heavily for Eisenhower's vice president, Richard Nixon, than men did. After all, it was John Kennedy who was something of a saber-rattler in comparison, charging that the Eisenhower Administration had allowed a missile gap between the United States and the USSR to develop, and taking a harder line on defending obscure islands off the coast of China.

Thus, in the mid-century decades women's differential preference for Republicans on the violence and war dimension roughly offset their preference for Democrats on the active government dimension. The emergence of an antiwar wing of the Democratic Party in the aftermath of U.S. involvement in Vietnam, however, changed the party's image. The Democrats came to be seen both as the more dovish of the two parties and the party more supportive of the welfare state, while the Republicans became the party with the more aggressive foreign and defense policy and the party hostile to the welfare state. As a consequence, differential gender preferences in the two clusters of issues now cumulate rather than offset as they did a generation ago.[28]

Although the preceding discussion of the gender gap might seem like something of a digression, it is quite relevant to the main line of our discussion. Commentaries on the culture war point to the gender gap as evidence that it exists: many women supposedly are offended by the "orthodox" position on morality and sexuality; consequently, their support for the "orthodox" (Republican) party has declined. But if the gender gap arises from traditional issues of peace and war and social welfare, and not from the issue of abortion in particular, or issues of morality or sexuality more broadly, then that is further evidence that talk of a culture war is a misconception.

Given such evidence how did the belief that abortion underlies the gender gap become so widespread? The explanation probably lies in Groucho Marx's famous quip "who are you going to believe—me or your own eyes?" Feminist groups—almost by definition led by women—have taken the lead in supporting abortion rights, while evangelical groups—usually headed by men—have taken the lead in opposing abortion.[29] Politicians, activists, and members of the media talk mostly to each other, so they make the natural but false assumption that the gender divide they see so clearly at the leadership level reflects a similar divide at the mass level.

---

[28] This realignment of party images gave rise to Chris Matthews's famous characterization of the Democrats as the "mommy" party and the Republicans as the "daddy" party. More recently, Berkeley linguist George Lakoff has argued that contemporary Republicans appeal to Americans who favor a "strict father" morality while Democrats appeal to those who prefer a "nurturant parent" morality. See *Moral Politics* (Chicago: University of Chicago Press, 2002).

[29] In addition, all Catholic priests are men.

Finally, it is also worth noting that the gender gap is not the result of women moving to the Democratic Party. That is another commonly believed myth. Rather, as a number of academic studies have noted, the gender gap primarily reflects the movement of men.[30] Men have moved away from the Democratic Party to the Republican Party, while the movement among women has been much smaller, as shown in Figure 5.11.[31] If the two parties are indeed engaged in a culture war, then Figure 5.11 suggests that over the past several decades, on balance more Americans have deserted than enlisted in the conflict.

EPILOGUE

On November 5, 2003 President Bush signed a bill outlawing so-called partial birth abortion except when necessary to save the life of the mother. Almost immediately cultural warriors opened fire. NARAL Pro-Choice America announced an ad campaign designed to meet the "greatest threat to abortion rights in three decades." According to NARAL President Kate Michelman,

Together these spots serve as a stark reminder of what could happen if we don't stop this tidal wave of antichoice activity

---

[30] See, for example, Daniel Wirls, "Reinterpreting the Gender Gap," *Public Opinion Quarterly* 50 (1986): 316–30; Barbara Norrander, "The Evolution of the Gender Gap," *Public Opinion Quarterly* 63 (1999): 566–76; Kaufmann and Petrocik, "The Changing Politics of American Men: Understanding the Sources of the Gender Gap," *American Journal of Political Science* 43 (1999): 880–81.

[31] To be precise, if leaning independents are treated as partisans, women show little change in their party identification over the past four decades, while men have moved away from the Democrats. If, as in Figure 5.11, leaning independents are treated as independents (as recommended by Warren Miller, one of the originators of the concept of party identification), then women have moved away from the Democratic Party, but at a slower rate than men. Warren Miller, "Party Identification, Realignment, and Party Voting: Back to the Basics," *American Political Science Review* 85 (1991): 557–568.

FIGURE 5.11

Men Have Left the Democratic Party Faster than Women Have

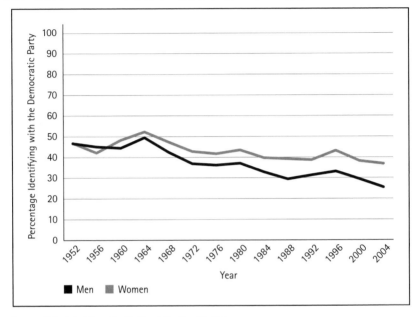

Source: Calculated from the National Election Studies.
Note: Partisans include strong and weak identifiers.

that is emanating right out of our own White House. The future health, safety and freedom of women in this country is in our hands. With antichoice leadership in Congress and the White House, and a razor-thin margin in the US Supreme Court, pro-choice Americans must act today to protect their rights tomorrow.[32]

Meanwhile, Troy Newman of Operation Rescue contemptuously dismissed the significance of the legislation:

[32] www.oregonnaral.org/s04politicalupdates/press/200306201.shtml, accessed November 11, 2003.

The new law signed by President G. W. Bush, similar to the bill twice vetoed by former President Bill Clinton, bans a narrowly defined act that is easily circumvented by the ever-crafty abortionist. It fallaciously includes a loop-hole exception to save the mother's life that many abortionists have routinely abused when included in other legislation.[33]

TV footage showed approving male representatives and senators watching President Bush sign the legislation, while disapproving women marched against the legislation, carrying signs and chanting slogans.

All of the myths about abortion and the culture war were on display here: extreme rhetoric, the contrasting genders of the pro-choice and pro-life spokespersons, and the contrasting genders of the legislative supporters and activist opponents. But beneath these images lay the larger underlying reality that polls have consistently shown that two-thirds of the American citizenry opposes partial birth abortion except when the health of the mother is at stake. Reflecting that brute fact, majorities in both chambers of Congress—Democrats as well as Republicans—voted for the bill. In prohibiting partial birth abortion except when the *life* of the mother is as stake, the bill actually went further than legislation that would have maximized popular support.[34] Perhaps for that reason, when the legislation was stayed by the courts, there was no great popular outcry against the decisions.

---

[33] operationrescue.org/ftd/PBA_Ban2003Nov6.asp, accessed November 11, 2003.
[34] An *NBC News/Wall Street Journal* poll conducted immediately (November 8–10) after the bill signing found Americans far less supportive of the new legislation (47 percent in favor, 40 percent opposed, 13 percent not sure) than previous polls would have led one to expect. Here again we see the typical pattern: pro-choice forces supported a weaker alternative than the average voter would have preferred, while pro-life forces supported a more restrictive alternative.

All in all, this particular episode confirms the general picture of abortion attitudes that we have described in this chapter: nuanced popular views of the issue reflected in majority approval of regulating some aspects of abortion, a gender gap among high-level political activists that is not apparent among ordinary Americans, and minimal partisan disagreement about the issue at the mass level contrasted with vitriolic conflict at the elite level.

As this second edition goes to press the Senate Judiciary Committee is conducting hearings on the nomination of John Roberts to the Supreme Court. While pro-choice interest groups have attempted to fan popular outrage toward the nomination, polls indicate that their efforts have largely failed. Indeed, one ad by NARAL was roundly condemned even by the supposedly liberal mainstream media.[35] For their part Democratic Senators appear to be doing little more than playing their expected roles in a by now well-rehearsed play. Perhaps the views of normal Americans on this issue have finally penetrated into the media and the more moderate segments of the political class.

---

[35] For example the *Los Angeles Times* characterized the ad as "patently dishonest" in a Sunday edition editorial. "Not Worth Fighting Over," *Los Angeles Times*, August 14, 2005: M4.

CHAPTER 6

A Closer Look at Homosexuality

In June of 2003 the U.S. Supreme Court issued *Lawrence v. Texas*, striking down a Texas statute outlawing sodomy. The decision reversed *Bowers v. Hardwick*, a controversial 1986 decision. While legal scholars generally agree that *Lawrence* called into question all laws regulating private consensual sexual relations—heterosexual as well as homosexual, the decision was widely regarded as a victory for gay and lesbian activists for whom reversing *Bowers* had been a crusade. The *Lawrence* decision provoked a firestorm of criticism from the activists in the trenches of the culture war:

> *This is a major wake-up call . . . . This is a 9/11, major wake-up call that the enemy is at our doorsteps.*[1]

> *Has the end of the world arrived because the Supreme Court ruled no state may prohibit private, consensual homosexual*

---

[1] The Reverend Louis Sheldon, chairman of the Traditional Values Coalition at www.townhall.com/news/politics/200306/CUL20030627a.shtml, accessed September 4, 2003.

conduct? No, the end of the world is being handled by the Supreme Judge. But the end of the Constitution has arrived, and that is something about which everyone in this temporal world should be concerned.[2]

Issues of homosexual behavior and homosexual rights have not been prominent on the national agenda for as long as abortion, although gays and lesbians began to come out of the closet and organize politically in the early 1970s, about the same time that abortion rose on the political radar screen. Some conflicts erupted over local antidiscrimination statutes, but the issue largely simmered on the back burner until a backlash developed in the 1980s. The stinging rebuke Congress handed President Clinton in 1993 after he proposed allowing openly gay Americans to serve in the military seemingly demonstrated the intense views held by many ordinary Americans on this issue, and many believed that *Lawrence* made homosexuality and homosexual rights a second major front in the culture war.

Yet after the decision there was no rioting in the streets, nor much in the way of protests and demonstrations. Antigay citizens did not mobilize and march on Washington, as the pro-life forces have done. Instead, one poll reported that while almost a third of registered voters thought the Supreme Court's *Lawrence* decision "a disaster," one-quarter said they did not really care, a fifth said the decision was not important although they did not like it, and the remaining fifth supported it.[3]

---

2 Cal Thomas, "End of the Constitution?" www.townhall.com/columnists/calthomas/printct2003 0701.shtml, accessed September 4, 2003.
3 Poll reported by Andres McKenna Research, conducted July 8–10, 2003, nationaljournal.com/ members/polltrack/2003/issues/03homosexuality.htm#3.

Supreme Court decisions—even highly publicized ones—are abstract developments to many Americans, however. A far more immediate example of changing public policy toward gays came in November of 2003 when the Massachusetts Supreme Court ruled that a ban on gay marriage violated the Massachusetts Constitution. In response, some town officials began issuing marriage licenses to gay and lesbian couples and some well-publicized marriages took place. In February of 2004, while the Massachusetts state legislature debated a constitutional amendment to ban gay marriage, Mayor Gavin Newsom of San Francisco ordered the county clerk to give marriage licenses to same-sex couples. Suddenly, gay marriage became the lead story on television and a front page story in the newspapers.

Antigay marriage activists proposed additional state bans on gay marriages, and Congressional Republicans proposed an amendment to the U.S. Constitution. In the November election antigay marriage initiatives (GMIs) passed in all eleven states where they appeared on the ballot, and some disappointed Democrats suggested that Gavin Newsom had reelected George W. Bush. In truth, there was little basis for such a conclusion. The publicity given the subject was out of all proportion to the concern that Americans felt. A February 2004 Gallup poll asked people to rank fourteen issues in order of their importance in the coming November election. Gay marriage came in fourteenth out of fourteen.[4] Moreover, there is little evidence that the issue played a major role in the 2004 election. But we are getting ahead of ourselves here. We come back to this subject below.

---

[4] Abortion came in thirteenth and gun control twelfth. What were the most important issues to most Americans who are not members of the political class? The economy, jobs, Iraq, terrorism, and health care. Gallup.

AMERICAN ATTITUDES TOWARD
HOMOSEXUALS AND HOMOSEXUALITY

Describing Americans' attitudes toward homosexuality is difficult because unlike the other topics discussed in this book, public opinion in this area has been changing fairly rapidly, and in contrast to the case of abortion, broad movements in public opinion are interrupted by reactions to current political events. We are attempting to describe a changing picture in this chapter, and it is too early to come to any firm conclusions about a subject that may well change during the coming years.

To begin, there is no denying that many Americans feel negatively toward gays and lesbians. For the past three decades the National Election Studies have included a measuring device called a "feeling thermometer," which asks people to assign a number that represents how warm or cold they feel about a group or person. The thermometer runs from 0 to 100 degrees, and respondents are told that they should treat 50 as the neutral point. Almost all groups receive a net positive rating—even welfare recipients, antiabortion activists, and "women's libbers" received an average rating a bit over 50 degrees in the years when those groups were included in the surveys. Despite the election result, in 2004 Republicans were rated 52 degrees and Democrats were rated 58.

Gays were unique in the 1980s in the number of people who gave them the coolest possible rating—zero, but as Figure 6.1 shows that number steadily declined, from almost a third in 1988 to less than 10 percent in 2000, before rising slightly in 2004 amid the controversy over gay marriage. Along with this sharp decline in extreme dislike, the average ratings of gays and lesbians have

FIGURE 6.1
Declining Hostility Toward Homosexuals

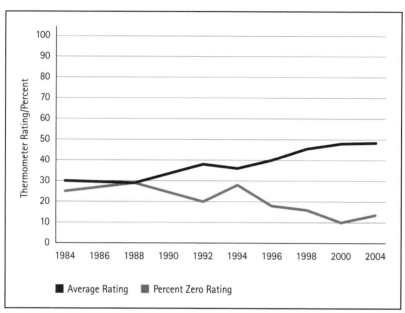

Source: Calculated from the National Election Studies.

climbed significantly in the past fifteen years. In the 1980s gays and lesbians were rated at 30 degrees or colder, a level of dislike exceeded only by "black nationalists" in the 1970s. By 2004 however, gays and lesbians were rated at 48.5 degrees, just a bit on the cool side of the neutral point. Blue state residents rated gays and lesbians at 52 degrees while red state residents rated them at 46 degrees, a difference more akin to a ditch than a chasm.

As is the case with abortion, majorities of Americans believe that homosexual relations are wrong. As shown in Figure 6.2, the General Social Surveys consistently find that a majority of Americans believes that sexual relations between two adults of the same

FIGURE 6.2

What About Sexual Relations Between Two Adults of the Same Sex?

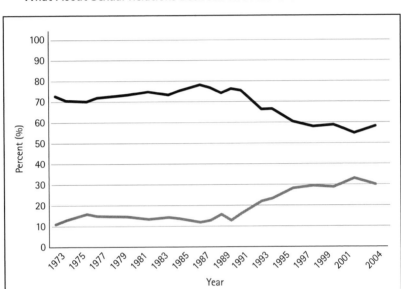

Source: Calculated from the General Social Surveys.

sex is wrong, although the size of the majority that believes this has declined from more than three-quarters to about 60 percent. But as with abortion, a significant number of Americans who believe homosexuality is wrong decline to criminalize it.[5] Figure 6.3 shows a significant swing in opinion between the mid-1980s and today. Less than two decades ago solid majorities of Americans felt that homosexual relations should be illegal, but even in the aftermath of the 2004 gay marriage furor, as many reject that proposition as accept it.

5 For a detailed discussion see Jeni Loftus, "America's Liberalization in Attitudes toward Homosexuality, 1973–1998," *American Sociological Review* 66 (2001): 762–82.

FIGURE 6.3
Should Homosexual Relations Between Consenting Adults Be Legal?

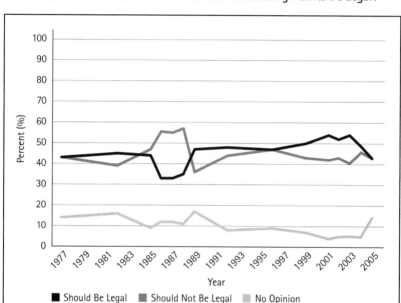

Source: The Gallup Organization.

Not only do Americans decline to criminalize behavior they believe to be immoral, they explicitly support protection of the rights of those they believe to be engaged in an immoral lifestyle. Even in the mid-1980s when a majority of Americans felt that homosexual relations should be illegal, majorities still supported civil liberties for gays,[6] and Figure 6.4 shows that the percentage of Americans who believe that gays and lesbians should have equal job opportunities has grown steadily since the 1970s to the point that there now is overwhelming support for equal employment

---

[6] In the 1984 and 1987 GSS surveys nearly 70 percent of respondents said that an admitted homosexual should be allowed to speak in public, and only 40 percent favored removing a book advocating homosexuality from the library.

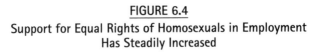

FIGURE 6.4

Support for Equal Rights of Homosexuals in Employment
Has Steadily Increased

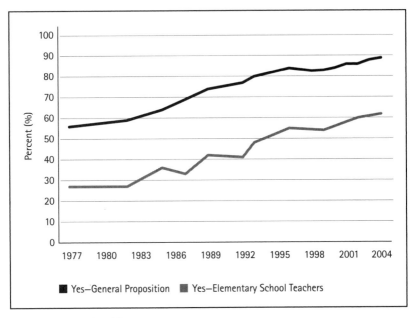

■ Yes–General Proposition   ■ Yes–Elementary School Teachers

Source: The General Social Survey.

opportunities for homosexuals, including majority support for
opportunities in occupations like teaching that as late as 1990
were considered too sensitive to permit the employment of homosexuals.

As with abortion, attitudes toward homosexuality differ across
various categories of the population, but the differences are
smaller than many might assume. Breakdowns of the Gallup data
plotted in Figure 6.3 show that men and women differ little. Similarly, whites and nonwhites differ little. The expected regional differences appear—there is about a 20 percent difference between
the orthodox South and the libertarian West in the percent who

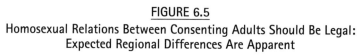

FIGURE 6.5
Homosexual Relations Between Consenting Adults Should Be Legal:
Expected Regional Differences Are Apparent

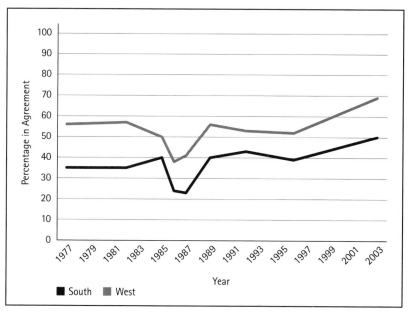

Source: The Gallup Organization.

would make homosexual relations legal, but even half the residents
of the South now express that view (Figure 6.5). Gallup does not
regularly subdivide Protestants into evangelical and mainline
denominations, nor ask about church attendance, so we cannot
systematically compare denominational and religiosity differences,
but a recent Gallup poll found that weekly churchgoers are only
half as likely to favor legalization of homosexual relations as those
who never attend church. Still, 40 percent of weekly churchgoers
favored legalization.[7]

---

[7] Gallup poll, July 25–27, 2003.

GAY MARRIAGE

In the 2004 election GMIs were on the ballot in eleven states and all passed. When combined with a poorly worded and even more poorly analyzed exit poll item that gave rise to an exaggerated "moral values" election interpretation, the claim that opposition to gay marriage elected George Bush gained a degree of plausibility. In truth, however, the gay marriage issue played little or no role in Bush's victory.

Both turnout and support for Bush were up pretty much across the board in 2004. Turnout in states with GMIs on the ballot was slightly higher than in states without such initiatives, but when other characteristics of the state were statistically taken into account, GMIs had no independent effect on turnout.[8] While the polls differ slightly, the modal finding is that evangelical Protestants and weekly churchgoers made up about the same proportions of the vote in 2004 as in 2000. Such a general increase in turnout suggests that it reflected the two parties' rediscovery of traditional get-out-the-vote methods (augmented by modern techniques to identify and target their likely voters) rather than the use of hot-button issues to motivate particular constituencies.

The vote for George Bush also increased across the board in 2004. Regrettably, the 2004 NEP exit poll asked whether voters considered themselves born-again or evangelical Christians, whereas the 2000 VNS exit poll asked whether voters self-identified as members of the religious right. A third of the electorate falls into

---

[8] Alan Abramowitz, "Terrorism, Gay Marriage, and Incumbency: Explaining the Republican Victory in the 2004 Presidential election," *The Forum* 2 (2004). Barry Burden, "An Alternative Account of the 2004 Presidential Election," *The Forum* 2 (2004).

the former category but only a fifth into the latter, so the categories are not directly comparable. But for what it is worth, the born-again constituency voted slightly less for Bush in 2004 than the religious right constituency did in 2000, consistent with the observation that not all evangelicals are social conservatives. A directly comparable category—weekly churchgoers—voted for the President at virtually the same rate in 2004 as in 2000. So, at a minimum it seems that GMIs did not swing a significantly larger proportion of religious Americans to the Republican camp. Table 6.1 lists some of the many categories of voters registering higher support for Bush in 2004 than in 2000, a list which includes African Americans, Hispanics, Jews, residents of the northeastern United States,

TABLE 6.1
Republican Gains in 2004 were Across the Board

GROUP	2000 BUSH VOTE	2004 BUSH VOTE	BUSH GAIN
Religious right*	68.2%	—	—
Born-again**	—	65.7	—
Regular churchgoers***	60.2	61.0	0.8
Non-churchgoers	40.8	42.0	1.2
African Americans	8.6	11.1	2.5
Hispanics	36.3	45.2	8.9
Jews	19.0	25.4	6.5
Northeasterners	41.3	43.9	2.6
Women	44.6	48.2	3.6

Source: 2000 VNS and 2004 NEP Exit Polls.

* "Do you consider yourself part of the conservative Christian political movement, also known as the religious right?"

** "Would you describe yourself as a born-again or evangelical Christian?"

*** Attend services weekly or more often.

people who do not attend church, and women—groups not normally associated with exceptional opposition to gay marriage.

Nevertheless, despite the lack of evidence that GMIs affected
the 2004 voting and considerable evidence of growing toleration
of homosexual relations and growing support for equal rights for
homosexuals, a majority of Americans continues to oppose gay
marriage. In the aftermath of *Lawrence* we examined eleven poll
items that asked about gay marriage.[9] Opposition ranged from 52
percent to 66 percent, with a median of 55 percent. Opposition to
civil unions or domestic partnerships was slightly lower—fourteen
polls reported a median opposition of 50 percent.

Polls conducted since the Massachusetts and San Francisco
developments show little change in this picture. If anything, opposition to gay marriage may have increased slightly. When given an
up-or-down choice between gay marriage and no legal recognition
of gay relationships, at least 60 percent of Americans oppose gay
marriage. When the option of civil unions is available, opposition
to legal recognition of gay relationships drops 10 to 20 percentage
points.[10] Table 6.2 lists some representative examples.[11]

On the other hand, as Table 6.3 shows, polls generally show
that support for a federal constitutional amendment to ban gay
marriage falls short of a clear majority. A significant number of
Americans who personally oppose gay marriage do not support a

---

[9] Some of these are contained in a very useful compilation of poll results by Karlyn Bowman, "Attitudes
about Homosexuality" (Washington, DC: AEI Studies in Public Opinion, updated December 11, 2003).
Others were found through an Internet search of various polling archives.
[10] The 2004 National Election Pool exit poll reported that 60 percent of voters favored either gay marriage or civil unions. If this figure is accurate, it indicates that opposition to gay marriage is lower among
people who actually voted than among all Americans or registered voters.
[11] The Quinnipiac University Poll consistently registers higher opposition to civil unions, perhaps
because of the question's suggestion that civil unions would be similar to marriage.

TABLE 6.2

Opposition to Gay Marriage and Civil Unions

"Do you think marriages between homosexuals should or should not be recognized by the law as valid, with the same rights as traditional marriages?" (Gallup, for CNN/USA *Today*)

Should not be: 63%   (average of five polls, February 2004–March 2005)

"Would you support or oppose a law that would allow same-sex couples to get married?" (Quinnipiac University Poll)

Oppose: 63%   (average of four polls, January 2004–December 2004)

"Do you strongly favor, favor, oppose, or strongly oppose allowing gays and lesbians to marry legally?" (Princeton Survey Research Associates, for Pew Research Center)

Oppose: 60%   (average of four polls, February 2004–October 2004)

"Which of the following arrangements between gay or lesbian couples do you think should be recognized as legally valid: same-sex marriages, civil unions but not same sex marriages, or neither same-sex marriages nor civil unions?" (Gallup for CNN and *USA Today*)

Neither: 44%   (average of two polls, November 2004, March 2005)

"Which comes closest to your view? Gay couples should be allowed to legally marry. OR, gay couples should be allowed to form civil unions but not legally marry. OR, there should be no legal recognition of a gay couple's relationship." (CBS News/*New York Times*)

No legal
recognition: 40%   (average of four polls, March 2004–November 2004)

"Would you support or oppose a law that would allow same-sex couples to form civil unions, giving them many of the legal rights of married couples?" (Quinnipiac University Poll)

Oppose: 53%   (average of four polls, January 2004–December 2004)

Source: Polling Report.com (pollingreport.com/civil/htm) accessed April 4, 2005.

TABLE 6.3
Popular Support for a Federal Constitutional Amendment
to Ban Gay Marriage

"Would you favor or oppose a constitutional amendment that would define marriage as being between a man and a woman, thus barring marriages between gay or lesbian couples?" (Gallup, for CNN/*USA Today*)

Favor: 52%   (average of five polls, February 2004–March 2005)

"Would you support or oppose amending the United States Constitution to ban same-sex marriage?" (Quinnipiac University Poll)

Support: 41%   (average of three polls, March 2004–December 2004)

"Do you think defining marriage as a union only between a man and a woman is an important enough issue to be worth changing the Constitution for, or isn't it that kind of issue?" (CBS News/*New York Times* Poll)

Important
Enough: 39%   (average of two polls, March 2004–November 2004)

"Would you favor or oppose an amendment to the U.S. Constitution saying that no state can allow two men to marry each other or two women to marry each other?" (National Annenberg Election Survey)

Favor: 42%   (average of three polls, February 2004–June 2004)

Source: Polling Report.com (pollingreport.com/civil/htm) accessed April 4, 2005.

constitutional amendment to ban it. The most likely explanation for their hesitation is that they simply do not believe that it is an important enough issue to merit a constitutional amendment. As we have noted at several points in this book, there is often a serious disconnect between the concerns of the political class and those of normal Americans. While gay marriage may be a major issue for many in the political class, it is a minor issue for most Americans. In a 2004 post-election survey Hillygus and Shields presented a large national sample with 16 issues and asked respondents to indicate the importance of each issue for their vote.[12] Even in the aftermath of the election—with its flurry of moral values commentary—respondents ranked gay marriage fifteenth out of sixteen issues in importance. Only tort reform scored lower.

In sum, the gay marriage issue is a good illustration of the point that even when Americans are closely divided, as they are on this issue, they are not as deeply divided as popular commentary claims.

THE FUTURE OF GAY RIGHTS ISSUES

Perhaps the politically most significant point to make about American attitudes toward homosexuality is the strong relationship such attitudes bear to age: while younger Americans are far less liberal than popular stereotypes suggest,[13] they are definitely more tolerant of homosexuals and more accepting of homosexual rights than older Americans. As Figure 6.6 shows, Americans of all ages have become more accepting, but older cohorts are dying off and being replaced by more tolerant younger cohorts. Of course, trend lines do not always continue in the same direction, as 1970s population scaremongers learned.[14] But we see no reason why the historical trend of steadily wider inclusion in the

---

[12] D. Sunshine Hillygus and Todd Shields, "Moral Issues and Voter Decision Making in the 2004 Presidential Election," *PS: Political Science & Politics* 38 (2005): 2001–2008.

[13] Christian Smith, with Melinda Denton, *Soul Searching: The Religious and Spiritual Lives of American Teenagers* (New York: Oxford University Press, 2005).

[14] According to various 1970s commentators, the world should have been enduring mass starvation for the past decade or so. Instead, contemporary commentators now are worrying about world population *implosion*. Compare Paul Ehrlich, *The Population Bomb* (Ballantine: 1968) with Phillip Longman, *The Empty Cradle: How Falling Birthrates Threaten World Prosperity and What do Do About It* (New York: Basic, 2004). Ben Wattenberg, *Fewer: How the New Demography of Depopulation Will Shape Our Future* (Ivan R. Dee, 2004). Straight line extrapolations of trends—economic, demographic, sociological, political—is a dangerous business.

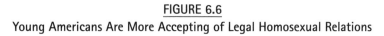

FIGURE 6.6

Young Americans Are More Accepting of Legal Homosexual Relations

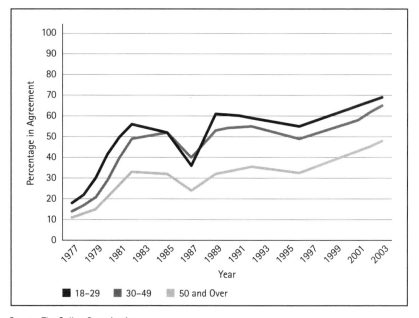

Source: The Gallup Organization.

Note: Some data points have been aggregated from divergent age categories due to inconsistent measurement over time.

American body politic will not continue in this case. If commandants on the "orthodox" side hope to win a culture war over homosexuality, they had better do it soon—their potential ranks are being thinned by mortality.

As we noted at the beginning of this chapter, public opinion on homosexuality is moving as a reflection both of long-term trends and short-term political developments. This makes it a dangerous issue for both parties, since political calculations made today may become outdated very quickly. In opposing gay marriage Republican elected officials seemingly are responding to the wishes of the majority of Americans, but in the party's support for a federal constitutional amendment they are going beyond what majorities of voters prefer, which probably explains why the Bush Administration has done so little to push such an amendment.[15] We think that the administration's political caution is understandable. While a majority of Americans is opposed to gay marriage and a plurality even to civil unions, fewer of them have any wish for a vitriolic conflict over the issue. Certainly, the recent history of antigay initiatives other than those concerning gay marriage provides little evidence that Americans are eager to endorse overtly antigay actions.[16] Moreover, given the direction in which opinion has been moving, and the greater support for homosexual rights among young people, any short-term political gains may well come with long-term costs if the Republicans become associated with antigay positions that are losing ground in the population.[17] At the present time Republicans and Democrats in the electorate differ on homosexuality, but as Figure 6.7 shows, even a bare majority of self-identified Republicans in 2003 favored legalization of homosexual relations, and independents—who hold the balance of electoral power—agree with Democrats on the issue.

As with abortion, there are obvious compromises that we think might attract the support of majorities of Americans—most

[15] A fact that has not gone unnoticed by social conservatives, e.g., W. James Antle III, "Republican Stepchildren (Message to social conservatives: Thanks for the votes. We'll call you in four years)," *American Conservative*, April 11, 2005.

[16] "Of eleven statewide initiatives from the last two decades that are readily classifiable as antigay, only three (27 percent) passed . . . . When referenda written by a legislature are considered with initiatives, the pass rate increases to 5 of 14 (38 percent) . . . ." Todd Donovan, Jim Wenzel, and Shaun Bowler, "Direct Democracy and Gay Rights Initiatives After *Romer*," in Craig Rimmerman, Kenneth Wald, and Clyde Wilcox, eds., *The Politics of Gay Rights* (Chicago: University of Chicago Press, 2000): 166.

[17] Certainly President Bush's initial reaction to proposed constitutional amendments prohibiting gay marriage was more cautious than the sentiments of the Republican base would have led one to expect. Susan Page, "Bush's Gay-Marriage Tack Risks Clash with His Base," *USA Today*, December 18, 2003: 6A.

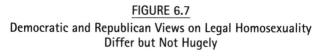

FIGURE 6.7

Democratic and Republican Views on Legal Homosexuality
Differ but Not Hugely

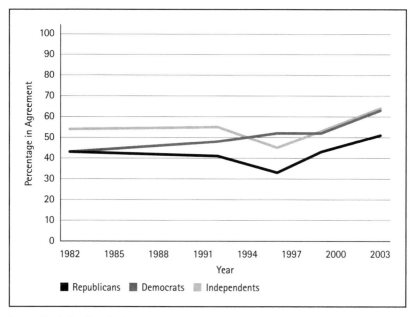

Source: The Gallup Organization.

obviously, the rights and duties of civil union without the name.
Various European countries have been moving in this direction.[18]
But we suspect that the views of activists on both sides of the issue
will make it difficult for such compromises to get on the agenda.
In frankness, however, there is not enough data to put these specu-
lations on a firmer basis.

[18] Sarah Lyall, "In Europe, Lovers Now Propose: Marry Me, a Little," *New York Times,* February 15,
2004: 3.

CHAPTER 7

Have Electoral Cleavages Shifted?

The preceding chapters have reported numerous tables and charts inconsistent with the claim that Americans are deeply divided. Public opinion data fail to support a portrait of "two big separate voting blocks." On the contrary, there is little evidence that the country is polarized even on "hot button" issues like abortion. On the whole the views of the American citizenry look moderate, centrist, nuanced, ambivalent—choose your term— rather than extreme, polarized, unconditional, dogmatic. But why, then, does there seem to be a significant change in electoral cleavages in recent elections?

Whereas elections once pitted the party of the working class against the party of Wall Street, they now pit voters who believe in a fixed and universal morality against those who see moral issues, especially sexual ones, as elastic and subject to personal choice.[1]

---

[1] Thomas Edsall, "Blue Movie," *Atlantic,* January/February 2003: 36.

What demographic factor separates voters more than any other? The answer is—religion . . . the two Americas evident in the 48 percent-48 percent 2000 election are two nations of different faiths. One is observant, tradition-minded, moralistic. The other is unobservant, liberation-minded, relativist.[2]

Even if citizen attitudes on most issues are not highly polarized, has the way such attitudes translate into votes changed? That is, even if Americans are not deeply divided on specific issues, could it be that their views translate into votes in new ways that somehow magnify the differences that exist? While we will show that traditional cleavages like economics by no means have disappeared—quite the contrary—we agree that new cleavages related to morality and religion now are more important than a generation ago. Thus, while the claim of a culture war is an exaggeration, the claim that politics has become more focused on religion and morality is accurate. The important question is whether the changing character of our politics reflects the changing positions and priorities of voters, or the changing positions, priorities, and strategies of the political class. The remaining chapters in this book argue the latter position.

THE RISE OF RELIGIOUS CLEAVAGES

Various scholars have noted that presidential votes and party identification correlate more closely with religion today than a generation ago.[3] In this context "religion" does not refer to

---

[2] Michael Barone, *Almanac of American Politics* (Washington DC: National Journal, 2002): 27–28.
[3] The most recent and comprehensive work is Geoffrey Layman, *The Great Divide* (New York: Columbia, 2001).

FIGURE 7.1

Deviation from Average Presidential Vote by Religious Group

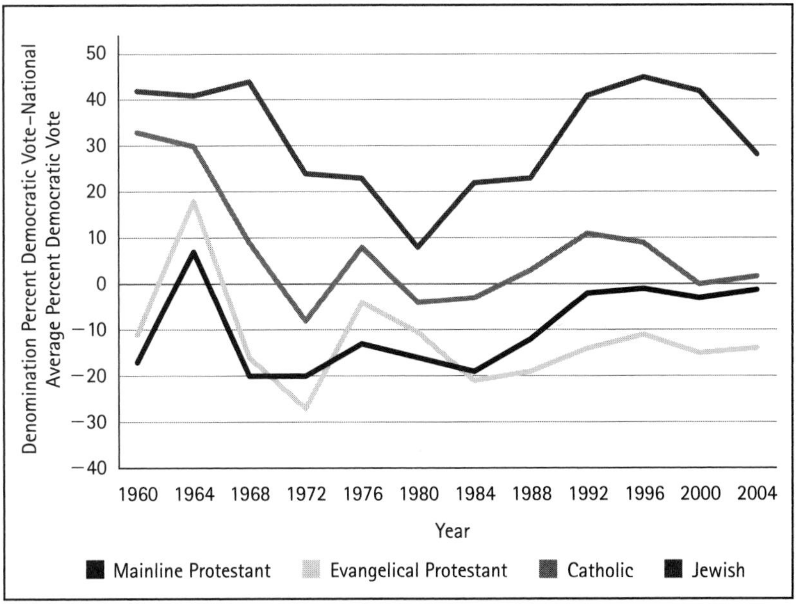

Source: Calculated from the National Election Studies.

denomination; rather, it refers to "commitment" or "religiosity."[4] As shown in Figure 7.1, the relationship between presidential vote and denomination has eroded over the past generation. Catholics, in particular, are far less dependably Democratic today than they were prior to 1972, and mainline Protestants are less dependably Republican than they were in the 1970s and 1980s. Of particular note is the reversal of mainline and evangelical voting patterns in 1984. Prior to that election mainline Protestants were more

---

[4] Robert Wuthnow, *The Restructuring of American Religion: Society and Faith Since World War II* (Princeton, NJ: Princeton Universitiy Press, 1988). Cf. Mark Brewer, *Relevant No More? The Catholic/Protestant Divide in American Electoral Politics* (Lanham, MD: Lexington Books, 2003).

Republican than evangelicals in every election save 1972—many southern Democrats at that time were white evangelicals. After 1984 evangelicals are increasingly more Republican than mainline Protestants. Of the major denominations, only Jews are as supportive of a single party—the Democrats—as they were at mid-century, although there was a significant erosion of Jewish support for Democratic presidential candidates beginning in 1972 that was not fully erased until 1992.

If the relationship between partisanship and denomination has eroded, the same cannot be said for the relationship between partisanship and religiosity or religious commitment. On the contrary, in recent elections the more religious an individual, the more likely he or she is to vote for and identify as a Republican.[5] For example, Table 7.1 contrasts degrees of religious commitment within two denominations that at one time were politically distinct. No more. Now Catholics and Baptists who regularly attend church are alike in their voting as are Catholics and Baptists who don't attend church. Denomination has faded in significance, but religiosity has not.

Has religiosity become a significantly more important correlate of American voting behavior than it was in past decades? The available data indicate that the answer is yes. The longest available measure of religious commitment is one of church attendance, available since 1952 in the National Election Studies.[6] We

---

[5] Geoffrey Layman, "Religion and Political Behavior in the United States," *Public Opinion Quarterly* 61 (1997): 288–316. Frank Newport, "Church Attendance and Party Identification," Gallup Poll Release, May 18, 2005.

[6] Religious commitment is a complex concept, to be sure, but church attendance is probably the most commonly used indicator. See the discussion in Karen Kaufmann, "The Partisan Paradox: Religious Commitment and the Gender Gap in Party Identification," *Public Opinion Quarterly* 68 (2004): 491–511.

TABLE 7.1
Holding Denomination Constant, More Religious People Voted More Republican in 2004

	BUSH VOTE
Baptists	
Attenders	55%
Nonattenders	34
Catholics	
Attenders	53
Nonattenders	33

Source: 2004 National Election Studies.

have examined the relationship between church attendance and the Democratic presidential vote and find an increasingly strong association between the two, albeit not one that grows linearly.[7] Figure 7.2 contrasts the voting behavior of the most and least religiously active Americans. Between 1964 and 1984 white regular churchgoers voted Republican at a significantly higher rate than nonchurchgoers, but the differences in these six elections amounted to only six or seven percentage points.[8] The partisan voting gap declined to an insignificant level in the Bush-Dukakis election of 1988, but in 1992 the voting gap between regular churchgoers and nonattenders exploded and has remained at levels higher than any seen in the four decades prior to 1992. Note, however, that while it remains high the religious gap has steadily *declined* since 1992: in particular, in 2004 the religious

[7] There were NES question format changes in 1970 and 1990 that create some problems for comparisons over time. For a full discussion see the appendix to this chapter.

FIGURE 7.2

Difference in Democratic Presidential Vote Between
Regular Churchgoers and Nonattenders

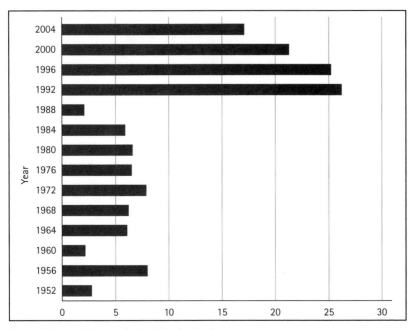

Source: Calculated from the National Election Studies.
Note: Includes white voters only.

gap was nearly 10 percentage points *lower* than in the two Clinton elections.

The stronger relationship between religiosity and voting that has developed recently appears to be genuine and not a spurious reflection of other factors. In Chapter 4 we described an earlier study of presidential voting aimed at explaining Al Gore's under-

---

[8] We have combined the "never attend" and the "attend a few times a year" categories as the "non-attenders" and the "attend weekly" and "attend almost weekly" as the "attenders." For the rationale see this chapter's appendix. The figure includes only white voters—since African Americans attend church regularly—and vote Democratic, including them hides the strength of the church-vote connection among whites.

performance in 2000. That study analyzed presidential votes from 1972 to 2000 as a function of party identification, ideological self-classification, presidential performance evaluations, economic evaluations, and candidate evaluations. To those comprehensive equations we added variables representing the five categories of church attendance. The results confirm the preliminary conclusions from the figures. Over and above standard (and powerful) predictors of the vote such as party, ideology, presidential performance, and candidate evaluations, in the past four elections (but not before) church attendance has had a highly significant (statistically speaking) association with presidential voting.

Figure 7.3 plots the deviation of the Democratic vote in the more extreme church attendance categories from the Democratic vote in that election. This rearrangement of the data suggests two additional observations. First, as the figure graphically emphasizes, the contemporary association between religion and presidential voting did not develop gradually. Rather, it emerged suddenly and dramatically in 1992. In Chapter 9 we speculate about the explanation for that sudden emergence. Second, although the resurgence of evangelical Christianity as a political force gets the lion's share of the news coverage as well as scholarly attention, at least in the realm of presidential voting, that resurgence is only part of the story. As Figure 7.3 shows, the other important part is the behavior of the unchurched. Their movement to the Democrats in 1992 counterbalanced the movement of weekly churchgoers to the Republicans, paralleling developments at the elite level,[9] and consistent with evidence that the movement of social

---

[9] Geoffrey Layman, "'Culture Wars' in the American Party System," *American Politics Quarterly* 27 (1999): 89–121.

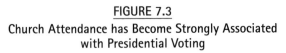

FIGURE 7.3

Church Attendance has Become Strongly Associated
with Presidential Voting

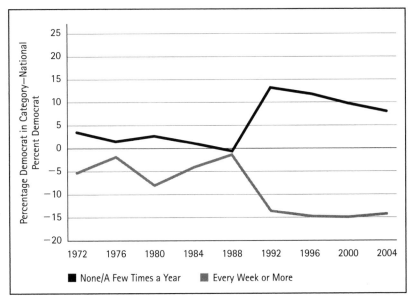

Source: Calculated from the National Election Studies.
Note: Includes white voters only.

conservatives to the Republicans has provoked a countermove-
ment of seculars to the Democrats.[10]

THE DECAY OF ECONOMIC CLEAVAGES?

So, religion in the sense of personal commitment has become a
more important cleavage in recent American elections, as propo-
nents of the culture wars thesis argue. But, do working class and

---

[10] Louis Bolce and Gerald De Maio, "Religious Outlook, Culture War Politics, and Antipathy toward
Christian Fundamentalists," *Public Opinion Quarterly* 63 (1999): 29–61.

Wall Street moralists now make common cause against blue-collar and Wall Street libertines, as Edsall suggests in the passage quoted earlier? Has the new cleavage of religion and morality eclipsed the old New Deal cleavage of class and income?[11] On the contrary, although religiosity has become more important, research finds little or no decline in the importance of economics. In fact, income divisions seem to be more politically relevant now than in earlier decades. McCarty, Poole, and Rosenthal report that both party identification and presidential vote have become *more closely* linked to income since 1972.[12] And Stonecash and Lindstrom report that Congressional elections outcomes have become more closely related to district income in recent decades.[13]

Some simple data make the point clearly. In Figure 7.4 we plot the difference in the presidential vote (percent Democratic minus percent Republican) between people in the highest and lowest thirds of the income distribution for the presidential elections since 1952.[14] Evidently, income has been a far more important correlate of the vote in recent decades than it was several decades ago. The partisan voting gap between lower and higher income voters in 2004 was the third largest in a half century (the largest if

---

[11] The religious cleavage is "new" only in a post-1928 view of American electoral history. The contemporary cleavage resembles the "Pietist-Liturgical" division that characterized much of American political history in the latter half of the nineteenth century. See, for example, Paul Kleppner, *The Third Electoral System, 1853–1892* (Chapel Hill: University of North Carolina Press, 1979).

[12] Nolan McCarty, Keith Poole, and Howard Rosenthal, *Income Redistribution and the Realignment of American Politics* (Washington, DC: AEI Press, 1997).

[13] Jeffrey Stonecash and Nicole Lindstrom, "Emerging Party Cleavages in the House of Representatives, 1962–1996," *American Politics Quarterly* 27 (1999): 58–88. Stonecash and Lindstrom find that the relationship between district income and election outcomes has grown stronger in northeastern, midwestern, and southern congressional districts (about three-fourths of the total), but not in mountain and western districts.

[14] The figure includes only white voters—since African Americans have low incomes and vote Democratic, including them exaggerates the strength of the income-vote connection among whites.

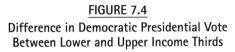

FIGURE 7.4
Difference in Democratic Presidential Vote
Between Lower and Upper Income Thirds

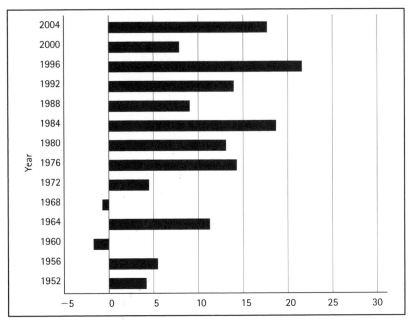

Source: Calculated from the National Election Studies.
Note: Includes white voters only.

African Americans are included). Interestingly, 2000 is the one
election that least fits the contemporary pattern: the economic gap
in 2000 was relatively small, closer to that in the 1950s than in the
Reagan and Clinton elections. In the first edition we commented
that this could be the start of a trend, or it could simply be an
aberration. The results of the 2004 election, which shows the
largest income gap among Republican and Democratic voters
than any election prior to 1984, supports the latter conclusion. On
the basis of one aberrant election some commentators concluded

that economics was no longer an important cleavage in American elections, a highly premature judgment that the 2004 election disproved.

Moreover, note that in recent elections the difference in Democratic presidential vote percentage between the highest and lowest thirds of the income distribution is nearly comparable to the difference in Democratic vote percentage between regular church attenders and those who do not attend services (compare Figure 7.2 and Figure 7.4). The glaring exception, of course, is 2000, where the religious difference is more than twice the economic difference, an occurrence that seems to have stimulated numerous claims that a new era had dawned in American politics.[15]

We do not wish to draw any firm conclusions about the relative importance of income and religious differences in contemporary elections. Such an estimate of relative importance would require a far more elaborate analysis than we have carried out, and analysts would argue at great length about the relative merits of measures and the most appropriate methods for analyzing the data. Moreover, as we explain in Chapter 9, the exercise may be impossible at this time. Suffice it to say that there is little systematic evidence that economics has disappeared or even weakened relative to religiosity.[16] Claims about the demise of economic

---

[15] Recall that the economy was near the end of an exceptional run in 2000, and that Al Gore chose not to run on the basis of the administration's economic performance.

[16] Consider a simple statistical analysis that predicts presidential vote as a function of income and church attendance. Formally, we estimate a dummy variable logit model in which Vote = a + b_1 (highest income third) + b_2 (lowest income third) + b_3 (weekly church attendance) + b_4 (no church attendance). Considering the elections since 1972, when the relationship between religiosity and presidential vote first appeared, eight of the sixteen coefficients on the religious variables are significant, and eight of the sixteen coefficients on the income variables are significant. Neither of the income dummy variables is significant in 1972 or 2000. Neither of the religious variables is significant in 1988.

cleavages in American elections are true only if one limits one's focus to the drop-off from 1996 to 2000. Anyone whose time horizon includes elections on either side of 2000 can continue to believe that the divide between the working class and Wall Street is deeper today than it was at mid-century.

APPENDIX TO CHAPTER 7

Measuring Religiosity

We use the NES church attendance variable to construct a temporally comparable measure of religiosity. But although the variable appears in every NES survey between 1952 and 2000, using it requires dealing with three different question formats. The three versions of the item are as follows:

1952–1968

[If the respondent expressed a religious preference] Would you say you go to church regularly, often, seldom, or never?

- Regularly
- Often
- Seldom
- Never

1970–1988

[If the respondent expressed a religious preference] Do you go to church (synagogue) every week, almost every week, once or twice a month, a few times a year, or never?

- Every week
- Almost every week
- Once or twice a month
- A few times a year
- Never

1990–2000

Lots of things come up that keep people from attending religious services even if they want to. Thinking about your life these days, do you ever attend religious services, apart from occasional weddings, baptisms, or funerals? [If "Yes"]: Do you go to religious services every week, almost every week, once or twice a month, a few times a year, or never?

- Every week
- Almost every week
- Once or twice a month
- A few times a year
- Never

These changes in question wording are associated with shifts in the responses they elicit. For instance, in 1990 the addition of two qualifying phrases altered the cue given to respondents. Instead of simply asking people how often they attended services, the question began by noting that many things "keep people from attending" services. Probably even more important, the question ruled occasional attendance at weddings, baptisms, and funerals out of consideration. Figure A7.1 plots the trends for "a few times a year" and "never," and the effect of the 1990 question wording change is obvious. On the assumption that church attendance patterns are fairly consistent across time, or at least that they do not change abruptly from year to year, it appears that respondents who had previously answered "a few times a year," began to answer that they "never" attended services when confronted with the revised item. Thus, to create a temporally comparable measure

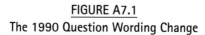

FIGURE A7.1
The 1990 Question Wording Change

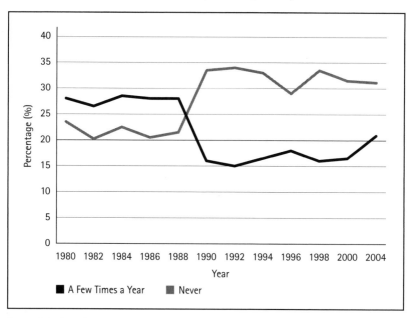

Source: Calculated from the National Election Studies.

from 1970 to the present we collapsed the two categories: "never" and "a few times a year" into a single category we label "non-attenders."

In 1970 not only did the question wording change, but the response categories did as well. Table A7.1 shows the distribution of church attendance across the four categories for 1968 and 1972. The far left-hand column shows the early question wording (1952–1968), and the far right-hand column shows the corresponding question wording for the later period (1970–1990). A comparison of the categories shows that they match up fairly

TABLE A7.1
Distribution of Church Attendance Reports by Pre- and Post-1970 Question Wording

EARLY QUESTION WORDING	1968	1972	LATER QUESTION WORDING
Never	12.1	16.5	Never
Seldom	34.6	29.6	A Few Times a Year
Often	15.4	15.7	Once or Twice a Month
Regularly	38.0	38.2	Every Week/Almost Every Week

Source: National Election Studies.

closely—particularly the categories "regularly" and "every week," and "often" and "once or twice a month."[1]

This gave us confidence that we could construct a time-series that would accurately capture church attendance patterns over time. Figure A7.2 plots our three-way categorization of church attendance from 1952 to 2000. Church attenders are those who reported going "regularly" from 1952 to 1968 and "every week" or "almost every week" thereafter. Nonattenders are those who reported no religious preference, "never," or "seldom" in the early period and "never" or "a few times a year" in the later period. The middle category consists of those who responded "often" in the early period and "once or twice a month" in the later period. This categorization produces a consistent time-series without sharp spikes or breaks (as those seen above in Table A7.1), and we

[1] The fact that the other categories do not match up as well is of less concern. Because of the 1990 question change those two categories are collapsed for our ultimate measure. Notice that when collapsing both categories the resulting measure is 46.7 percent not attending in 1968 and 46.1 percent not attending in 1972.

FIGURE A7.2
A Consistent Categorization of Church Attendance

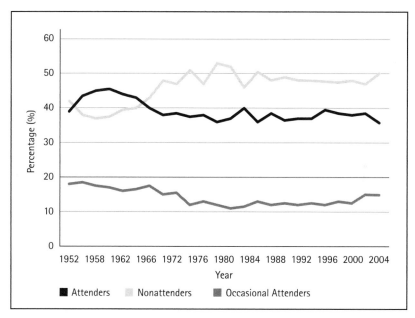

Source: Calculated from National Election Studies.

are therefore reasonably confident that this categorization of answers to the varying church attendance questions is the best available measure of religiosity for the period from 1952 to 2004.

CHAPTER 8

The 2004 Election and Beyond

As the returns streamed in on election night and Democratic hopes slipped away, the attention of the political class turned from the race itself to allotting credit and blame for the outcome. By the time the sun rose on the east coast the commentariat had decreed that "moral values" reelected George W. Bush. Social conservatives happily took credit, a perfectly normal reaction—constituencies on the winning side regularly declare that their support was crucial in order to lay claim to the largest possible share of the spoils of victory. At the same time, disappointed liberals uncritically accepted the initial story line. This too was a perfectly normal reaction. By painting Bush voters as a homogeneous body of Bible-thumping, evolution-denying, bigoted yahoos, the liberal minority was able to maintain its belief in its intellectual and moral superiority.

But liberals would have done better to analyze rather than emote. The moral values interpretation of the election had a flimsy

TABLE 8.1
The NEP Exit Poll Item

MOST IMPORTANT ISSUE	
Taxes	5.2%
Education	4.4
Iraq	14.7
Terrorism	18.9
Economy/Jobs	19.7
Moral Issues	21.8
Health Care	8.0

Source: NEP, 13,719 respondents.

foundation. It arose from a single survey item included on the exit poll conducted by the National Election Pool (NEP). The question read, "What one issue mattered most to you in deciding how you voted for president?" Respondents were offered seven choices. Table 8.1 lists their responses.

A survey analyst hardly knows where to begin qualifying any conclusions based on the responses to this question:[1]

1. Even with nearly 14,000 respondents, and even if everything else about the item was beyond question, few analysts would confidently say that the 22 percent who chose moral values actually were more common in the electorate than the 20 percent who chose economy/jobs or the 19 percent who chose terrorism. If one had to draw a conclusion from this data, the only appropriate one would be that

[1] As pointed out immediately after the election by Gary Langer, director of polling for ABC. "A Question of Values," *New York Times*, November 6, 2004, nytimes.com.

responses were quite scattered with no single issue driving the presidential vote.[2]

2. "Moral values" is a category, a collection of issues that potentially contains numerous specific examples. In contrast, the other alternatives are single issues. If one were to combine Iraq and the war on terrorism (the Bush administration maintained they were one and the same) into a single "security" category, that category would contain 34 percent, half again as many responses as in the moral values category. Similarly, if one were to combine taxes, economy/jobs, and health care into a "domestic economic issues" category, that category contains 33 percent, 50 percent more responses than moral values.

3. Alternatively, rather than create broader issue categories more comparable to the category, moral values, one could deconstruct the category moral values.[3] Probably because of the media sound and fury about GMIs and Republican campaign emphasis on their evangelical base, the meaning of moral values was quickly equated with gay marriage and abortion. That equation was unjustified. In a postelection survey the Pew Research Center repeated the NEP item to one-half of a national sample. The other half received no list of answers—they were asked to reply in their own words. The half-sample that received the list chose moral values 27 percent of the time, a bit higher than

---

[2] At a post-election conference held at Stanford University, a Republican pollster commented that when the data came across his desk, he didn't notice the moral values responses. What struck him was the small number of people choosing "taxes," the core issue of the Republican Party since Ronald Reagan.
[3] Given many liberals' affection for deconstruction, it is surprising that more of them did not take this route.

the election-day sample, but understandable given that the survey occurred during the midst of the post-election furor about moral values. But in the half-sample that replied in their own words, only 2 percent said gay marriage, 3 percent said abortion, and 9 percent said moral values generally, suggesting that people used the category to voice concerns broader than gay marriage and abortion.[4]

4. People vote on the basis of considerations other than policy issues. Their votes reflect long-standing party allegiances, general ideological leanings, and their appraisals of the records, personalities, capacities, and characters of the candidates. When an incumbent runs for reelection past performance is particularly important—the four-year record is a much more concrete factor to many voters than promises of what the candidates propose to do about health care, declining test scores, tax reform, and other policy issues. In 2004 the *Los Angeles Times* also conducted an exit poll. It included an item whose wording was more general than the NEP item: "What did you like most about your choice for president?" Responses appear in Table 8.2. Had the NEP included this item, the storyline would have been different (and much closer to the truth): the election hinged on presidential leadership and security concerns. The president's biggest advantage over John Kerry lay in those areas and his perceived honesty/integrity. Note that similar proportions of Bush and Kerry voters chose "shares my values."

---

4 "Four More Years," pollingreport.com/2004.htm, accessed November 16, 2004.

TABLE 8.2

The Los Angeles Times

"What did you like most about your choice for president?" (2 replies coded)

	BUSH VOTERS	KERRY VOTERS
Strong leader (37%)	55%	18%
Shares my values (22%)	24	21
Cares about people like me (21%)	17	26
Honesty and integrity (21%)	27	15
Keep me safe from terrorism (13%)	19	6
Overall political ideology (13%)	6	20
Build respect for U.S. (13%)	4	23

Source: *The Los Angeles Times*, 5,154 respondents.

In sum, the initial interpretation of the election was a classic example of "pack journalism." What was particularly disappointing is that many media commentators are sufficiently knowledgeable about public opinion surveying to have recognized the problems noted above. Nevertheless, they joined the pack and promulgated a misleading interpretation of the election.

None of this is to deny that moral values were an important—even dominant—concern for some Americans in 2004. Much to the dismay of liberals, more than a few Americans even rank such considerations higher than their personal material welfare.[5] But the evidence suggests that "moral values" (1) incorporates more issues and concerns than just gay marriage and abortion, and (2) played a much smaller part in the 2004 election than initially proclaimed by many and still believed by some.

---

[5] Robert Frank, *What's the Matter with Kansas?* (New York: Metropolitan Books, 2004). Those who rank moral values higher than economics are not the poorer Americans, however. See Larry Bartels, "What's the Matter with *What's the Matter with Kansas?*" www.princeton.edu/~bartels/kansas.pdf.

THE 2004 VOTING

If the electoral contribution of moral values was exaggerated in 2004, then what were the factors that propelled President Bush to a second term? Before offering an answer the first thing that should be said is that relative to the historical record, President Bush ran more poorly than expected for a president seeking reelection in a period of relative prosperity. He received 51.2 percent of the two-party popular vote, a margin of 2.4 percent over John Kerry. One widely cited statistical model based only on party, incumbency, and economic fundamentals predicted that the president's margin would be 15 percent of the two-party vote![6] Another model that incorporates war casualties predicted a much smaller margin—almost 6 percent, but one still more than twice as large as the actual margin.[7] An assortment of other, more complicated models that included polling data from much closer to the election produced a median forecast of 53.8 percent of the two-party vote for the president—a margin (7.6 percent) three times as large as the actual margin.[8] For all the talk of the brilliance of the Republican campaign, the election was closer than would have been expected from historical experience.[9]

---

[6] fairmodel.econ.yale.edu/vote2004/index2.htm.

[7] www.handels.gu.se/~econdhib/election2004.htm.

[8] James Campbell, "Introduction—The 2004 Presidential Election Forecasts," *PS: Political Science and Politics* 37 (2005): 733–35.

[9] Although there is no way to prove it, our view is that had Bush chosen more moderate courses of action after the successful war in Afghanistan (no invasion of Iraq, no additional tax cuts, no support of proposals widely viewed as anti-environment, no gay marriage amendment), he could have won reelection with a margin closer to Clinton's in 1996 or Reagan's in 1984 than to his actual margin. Consistent with this hunch Abramowitz and Stone report that ". . . the higher a state's turnout in 2004, the *lower* Bush's vote share in a state . . . . This finding suggests that the polarized nature of Bush's candidacy may have energized the opposition even more than it did his own base." Alan Abramowitz and Walter Stone, "The Bush Effect: Polarization, Turnout, and Activism in the 2004 Presidential Election." Paper presented at the 2005 Annual Meetings of the American Political Science Association, Washington, DC.

Most campaigns claim that the election will be close in order to keep their workers and supporters motivated, but although only hearsay, our conversations with people close to the Bush campaign suggested that they did in fact believe that the statistical forecasts were over-optimistic. Several bits of data were troubling to the campaign. The president's job approval ratings were lower than those of any reelected president since such data became available.[10] In addition, as Figure 8.1 shows, the widely followed "direction of the country" survey item indicated that a majority of Americans believed the country was on the wrong track (a belief that persisted after the election as well). Thus, as the election approached, the collective electorate was not at all certain about whether to continue George W. Bush in office. Why did a majority of them decide to do so, if the "moral values" explanation was not the reason?

Aggregate election returns identify some likely suspects. As noted in Chapter 6, the vote for the president rose across-the-board, although only slightly: George Bush increased his proportion of the vote in 32 of the 50 states. Abramowitz points out that the Republican vote increased about the same amount in states Bush carried in 2000 and states that Gore carried in 2000, in states experiencing below average unemployment, and in states experiencing above average unemployment, in states without GMIs on the ballot and in states with them.[11] Although it is logically possible that a general gain like this reflected similarly-sized but differently-caused gains in numerous different groups, a general surge

---

[10] Jeffrey Jones, "Bush's Re-Election Prospects Unclear From Historical View," Gallup Poll Release, June 29, 2004.
[11] Alan Abramowitz, "Terrorism, Gay Marriage, and Incumbency: Explaining the Republican Victory in the 2004 Presidential Election," *The Forum* 2 (2004). www/bepress.com/forum.

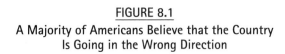

FIGURE 8.1

A Majority of Americans Believe that the Country
Is Going in the Wrong Direction

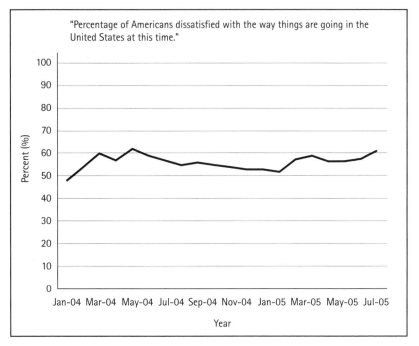

"Percentage of Americans dissatisfied with the way things are going in the
United States at this time."

Source: The Gallup Organization.

more than likely reflects the effects of a factor that operates on a
large, widely-distributed segment of the electorate.[12] The economy is the most common such factor, and indeed, it was an important factor in the 2004 voting. Another such general factor is
homeland security and fear of terrorism. As Abramowitz observes:

> *There was, however, one exception to the rule of consistent
> gains for George Bush between 2000 and 2004. Mr. Bush*

---

[12] Barry Burden, "An Alternative Account of the 2004 Presidential Election," *The Forum* 2 (2004).
www.bepress.com/forum.

gained an average of 5.4 percentage points in the three states most directly affected by the September 11th terrorist attacks— New York, New Jersey, and Connecticut—compared with 2.5 percentage points in the rest of the country.[13]

A close look at the demographic groups that increased their support for George Bush between 2000 and 2004 offers further support for the importance of homeland security concerns in the 2004 election. In Chapter 6 we pointed out that Bush gained among groups such as Jews, Latinos, non-churchgoers, and women, categories ordinarily not considered part of the social conservative base (Table 6.1). Women are especially interesting here. Given that they comprise a majority of the electorate and are widely spread across the country, any change in the vote of women would produce an across-the-board surge. That appears to be what happened in 2004. The gender gap closed up in 2004. It did so not because of decreased support for Bush among men; rather, women accounted for all of the surge to Bush. The various exit polls reported that women voted for Bush at a rate approximately 5 percentage points higher in 2004 than in 2000. This shift within such a large category overshadows any gains that could be attributed to social conservatives. Had women voted for John Kerry in the same proportions that they voted for Al Gore in 2000, in all likelihood Kerry would now be president.

Of course, it could logically be the case that it was precisely socially conservative women who moved toward Bush, but we know of no one who has made that argument. More importantly, if we look at the move to the president among women, it appears

---

13 Ibid., p. 6.

TABLE 8.3
The 2004 Republican Swing Among Women Was General

	2000	2004	GAIN
Black Women	5.8%	9.8%	4.0%
Latina Women	34.9	41.4	6.5
White Women	50.5	55.5	5.0
Married Black Women	7.1	11.5	4.4
Married Latina Women	37.3	43.8	6.5
Married White Women	54.9	61.8	6.9
Married W W with Children	58.9	66.0	7.1
Married W W without Children	51.5	59.4	7.9
Unmarried W W with Children	40.6	47.1	6.5
Unmarried W W without Children	40.3	43.1	2.8

Source: NEP

that it was an across-the-board surge. Some analyses have emphasized subcategories of women—white women, married women, married women with children—but Table 8.3 suggests that these distinctions are only variations on the major theme.[14] Women surged to Bush—white and minority women, married and unmarried women, women with children and women without them. Although the numbers begin to get small when we go to finer and finer categories, the only category that seemed resistant to the Republican appeal was unmarried white women without children. In all likelihood the horrific events of 9/11 shook the

[14] We say "suggests" rather than "shows" because there are some ambiguities in classifying women in the NEP. Respondents were only asked, "Are you currently married?" And, "Do you have any children under 18 living in your household?" Thus, a recently widowed woman who had just sent her last child off to college might be classified as childless and unmarried in the NEP. The NES asks a series of more precise questions, but given the much smaller number of respondents and the problem of over-reporting votes, the numbers are too small to draw firm conclusions.

traditionally more pacifistic, more antiviolence attitudes of women, producing the narrower gender gap and the Bush surge.[15]

Professional social scientists would consider much of the preceding evidence suggestive but not conclusive, because the importance of the individual factors we have considered has not been statistically estimated with all other relevant factors held (statistically) constant. Fortunately, we do not have to rev up any complicated statistical machinery here because others already have done so. Abramowitz reported an analysis of state-level aggregate data that examines the 2004 vote for Bush as a function of his 2000 vote in the state, the presence of a gay marriage initiative on the ballot, the increase in state turnout between 2000 and 2004, the unemployment rate in the state, and a special variable for New York, New Jersey, and Connecticut, the three states most directly touched by the 9/11 attacks. He finds that the 2000 vote for Bush carried over almost perfectly to 2004, the unemployment rate and GMIs had no effect, the 9/11 states were almost 3 percentage points more likely to vote for Bush, and perhaps surprisingly, Bush did more poorly in the states with higher turnout.[16]

In the most extensive analysis to date, Hillygus and Shields identify the factors determining the 2004 voting more directly and precisely by analyzing a large (> 2000 voter) post-election survey conducted by Knowledge Networks. Consistent with earlier polls, they report that voters assigned only moderate importance to abortion and little importance to gay marriage—ranking the latter fifteenth out of sixteen issues, higher only than tort reform. Moreover, voters who disagreed with their candidate's positions on

[15] Karen O'Connor, "For Better or For Worse? Women and Women's Rights in the Post 9/11 Climate," in *American Government in a Changed World* (New York: Longman, 2003): 180–81.
[16] Abramowitz, "Terrorism, Gay Marriage, and Incumbency."

these issues were much less likely to defect from their partisan allegiance than those who disagreed with their candidate's stance on economic issues or the war in Iraq and terrorism. Holding everything else constant, Hillygus and Shields find that the Iraq war, terrorism, and perceptions of the economy were the dominant influences on the vote, exerting their effects across the board. Views on abortion and gay marriage registered significant effects, but only among southern voters. Their large voter sample enables Hillygus and Shields to subdivide it to see if the statistical conclusions vary across regions, among political independents, in the battleground states, and in states with GMIs on the ballot. Their conclusions bear quoting in full:

> *Ultimately, the values voter explanation appears to be only a very minor part of citizens' voting calculus in the 2004 presidential election . . . . Among the most decisive groups—Independents and respondents in battleground states—gay marriage and abortion had no impact on individual vote choice once other factors were controlled. Only in the South did the values issue of gay marriage have an impact on individual vote choice; yet few ever doubted the strength of the GOP, nor Bush's electoral lead, in the South. Even here, the importance of other issues dwarfed the impact of attitudes toward gay marriage and abortion. It appears that values-based appeals only served to reinforce Bush's support among those already planning to vote for him, but failed to persuade new voters.*[17]

---

[17] D. Sunshine Hillygus and Todd G. Shields, "Moral Issues and Voter Decision Making in the 2004 Elections," *PS: Political Science and Politics* 38 (2005): 201–209.

In sum, elections are complicated affairs, but the available evidence indicates that the deciding factors in the 2004 voting had far more to do with presidential leadership and with overarching issues like the war in Iraq and the ability to keep the country safe from further terrorist violence than with issues like abortion and gay marriage that are critical only to small minorities of Americans. The Bush campaign maintained a relentless focus on terrorism and national security and insisted that the war on terror and the war in Iraq were one and the same. While a significant proportion of Americans felt uncertain about the latter equation, enough were sufficiently uncertain about John Kerry's ability to lead the country through dangerous times that they decided to stick with the incumbent.

Finally, if one wanted to assign the credit or pin the blame for reelecting George Bush on a particular group, it would not be social conservatives, it would be women. Rather than excoriate red state Americans, Maureen Dowd and Jane Smiley should have screamed at the mothers, sisters, and daughters of America.

POSTSCRIPT: BEYOND 2004

In March 2005, a short four months after the election, the political class fought another skirmish in the culture war over the tragic situation of a young woman, Terri Schiavo, then in the fifteenth year of a "persistent vegetative state" following cardiac arrest in 1990. Her husband contended that although she left no living will, his wife had verbally expressed a wish not to be kept alive in such a state. In 1998 Mr. Schiavo sought court permission to disconnect the feeding tube that kept Ms. Schiavo alive. Her parents ardently opposed his petition. State courts repeatedly held for her husband, and despite vigorous efforts by Florida Governor Jeb Bush, the matter appeared to be near an end.

The end was prolonged, however, by political intervention. A Republican Senate staffer wrote a controversial memo urging Congressional Republicans to intervene in the Schiavo case because it would be "a great political issue" particularly in the effort to defeat Florida Democratic Senator Bill Nelson in 2006.[18] The influence of the memo is unknowable, but whether their motivations were strategic or sincere, House and Senate Republicans acted, passing a bill to transfer the Schiavo case to federal court. President Bush interrupted his vacation to fly back to Washington and sign the bill. Meanwhile, nervous Democrats (apparently still believing in the moral values interpretation of the 2004 election) lay low.

In the next few weeks the disconnect between the political class and the rest of America became strikingly evident. Far from good politics, numerous polls showed that majorities of Americans agreed with the state (and ultimately the federal) courts' decisions to permit removal of the feeding tube. The op-ed pages and the blogosphere teemed with intense discussions of the polls, charging that poll questions were loaded against Shiavo's case (most polls) or toward her case (mainly Zogby), and debating the meaning and descriptive accuracy of terms like persistent vegetative state, coma, life-support, and so forth. Additionally, factors unique to the particular case such as the motivations of Ms. Schiavo's husband and

---

[18] A staffer by the name of Brian Darling took the fall for writing the memo. His boss, Senator Mel Martinez claimed never to have read the memo, only that he had "inadvertently passed it" on to Senator Thomas Harkin.

parents affected responses to poll questions. Question wording and framing can make a significant difference of course, but any fair consideration of the collection of survey evidence points to the conclusion that a majority of Americans felt that Ms. Schiavo should be allowed to die.[19]

Even more clearly, a large majority of Americans disapproved of federal intervention in the case and believed that the motivation for the intervention was political.[20] In their view the Congress and the president should not have gotten involved and the federal courts properly declined to get involved. Even a large majority of Republicans disapproved of the attempted political intervention.[21]

Such evidence surprised many in the media and in the political class, although it should not have surprised readers of this book. Ms. Schiavo's supporters in this noisy but narrow skirmish framed it as a battle between those who believed in a "culture of life," which holds all life inherently and equally sacred, and those "in love with death."[22] Between two such positions there could be no compromise.[23] But as with another "life" issue—abortion—the vast majority of Americans saw it differently from the culture warriors, agreeing with *both* sides of the argument. Indeed, all life is precious, but there are some conditions under which the best course is to allow it to end. Rather than adhere to a bright-line principle, Americans once again revealed their pragmatic mentality, preferring to make decisions on a case-by-case basis, and

---

19 "Terri Schiavo," pollingreport.com/news.htm, accessed April 11, 2005.
20 Ibid.
21 Lydia Saad, "Congress Gets Thumbs Down for Stepping Into Schiavo Case," Gallup Poll Release, April 7, 2005.
22 Peggy Noonan, "In Love With Death," www.wsj.com, March 24, 2005.
23 "When a society comes to believe that human life is not *inherently* worth living, it is a slippery slope to the gas chamber. You wind up on a low road that twists past Columbine and leads toward Auschwitz." (emphasis in original) Ibid.

believing that such decisions should be left to families, not deter-mined by government. In this case, Bush re-election strategist Matthew Dowd did not see "80 to 90 percent of the country look-ing at each other like they are on separate planets." Instead, he correctly saw that ". . . the vast majority of Americans . . . thinks this is a very difficult situation. They are glad they don't have to make the decision that is involved, and they don't see it as some-thing they want to be forced to have a political dialogue about."[24]

In and of itself, we do not believe that the Schiavo case will do significant damage to the electoral prospects of Republicans. But as with gay and lesbian issues, there is a long-term electoral dan-ger to a party that consistently takes polar positions on controver-sial issues, especially one that may well lose further popular sup-port in the future. A majority of Americans believes in euthanasia in principle (Figure 8.2), and as the baby boom generation ages more and more families will be confronted with tragic choices such as those present in the Schiavo case.[25] We suspect that public opinion on this issue will come to resemble that on abortion and homosexuality: even many of those who consider such choices immoral will not support government efforts to prohibit them.

At the other end of life—the beginning—another set of issues has recently emerged: embryonic stem cell research. The science is advancing rapidly, the issue itself is complex, there clearly are sig-nificant ethical questions to consider, and we doubt that Ameri-

---

[24] Quoted in Ronald Brownstein, "'Culture of Life' Issues Split GOP," www.latimes.com, March 28, 2005.

[25] David Moore, "Three in Four Americans Support Euthanasia." www.gallup.com/poll/content??ci=16333. The reason for the consistently higher support for euthanasis as compared to doc-tor-assisted suicide is not obvious. Interestingly, in the poll of May 2–5, 2005, 61 percent of Evangelical Christians approved euthanasis, but only 32 percent approved of doctor-assisted suicide.

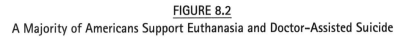

FIGURE 8.2

A Majority of Americans Support Euthanasia and Doctor-Assisted Suicide

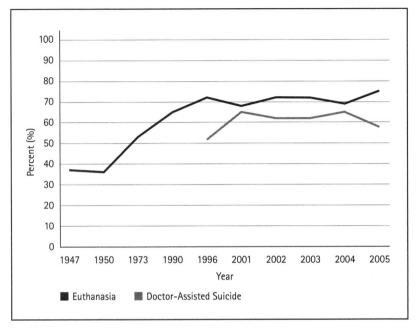

Source: The Gallup Organization.

cans' views are as well-formulated as their views on end-of-life issues. All that said, at the present time a majority of Americans believes that research using embryonic stem cells is moral (Figure 8.3). While support is significantly stronger among Democrats and Independents, Republicans are evenly split on the morality of such research, and a large minority approves of such research.[26]

---

[26] On the morality of such research see Frank Newport, "Joseph Carroll, "Party Lines Shape Views of What's Morally Acceptable," Gallup Poll Release, May 24, 2005. On support of such research see "Stem Cell Research," CBS News Poll, May 24, 2005.

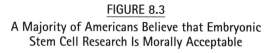

FIGURE 8.3

A Majority of Americans Believe that Embryonic
Stem Cell Research Is Morally Acceptable

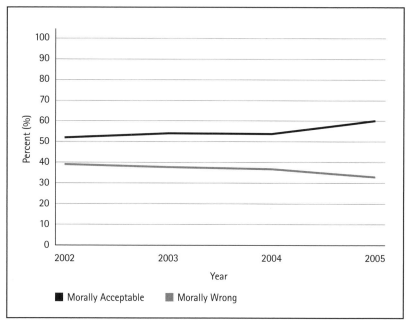

Source: The Gallup Organization.

Even the Republican base is not as homogeneous as usually assumed, with more than a third of white Evangelicals and weekly churchgoers approving of such research.[27] Not everyone who approves of such research approves of federal funding of the research, of course—there is a 20 percentage point gap between approval of the research in principle and approval of extending federal funding to more stem cell lines. Thus, we might expect to see some members of Congress take a position analogous to that

[27] "Stem Cell Research."

taken on abortion—supporting the principle, but opposing public funding.

In May of 2005 fifty House Republicans joined a large majority of Democrats to pass a bill expanding federal funding of stem cell research. A majority of the Senate also appeared ready to support expanded funding, but President Bush, professing his commitment to a "culture of life" threatened to veto it if it reached his desk. In late July Senate Majority Leader and likely 2008 presidential candidate Bill Frist (R-Tenn.) announced that he supported the House legislation and would bring it to the floor, a decision that insured passage, although not by a large enough majority to override a veto. Some observers suggested that Frist was trying to make up for his somewhat embarrassing involvement in the Schiavo case, but whether his reasons were sincere of strategic, Frist was putting himself on the side of a national majority, although at the cost of support from some elements in the Republican base.[28]

In sum, public opinion on both beginning of life and end of life issues probably is in a state of evolution. But what seems clear is that on both kinds of issues a majority does not support an absolute "culture of life" position, nor an "anything goes" position, not because their views are unconsidered, but because like abortion, they view the issues as complex and not easily given to black and white answers. Americans believe neither that embryos should be manufactured without restriction nor that research using embryonic stem cells should be prohibited. They believe neither that we should casually pull the plugs on our irreparably

---

[28] Frist, whose specialty is heart-lung transplants, had ventured a diagnosis of Ms. Schiavo's mental condition after viewing a videotape. His statement was widely criticized and generally interpreted as a transparent attempt to curry favor with social conservatives in the Republican base.

damaged fellow citizens, nor that we should keep them alive indefinitely when all hope is gone. Americans will resist efforts to make them choose between one pole or the other of the debate, a likely source of future frustration to political activists in this arena.

CHAPTER 9

Reconciling Micro and Macro

The previous chapters have shown that the evidence for a culture war at the level of ordinary Americans is underwhelming. There is little indication that voters are polarized now or that they are becoming more polarized—even when we look specifically at issues such as abortion that supposedly are touchstone issues in the culture war. On the contrary, there is even evidence that public opinion has grown more centrist on such issues and more tolerant of the divergent views, values, and behavior of other Americans. Despite the close results of recent national elections the country is not deeply divided. All of this data suggests that, for better or for worse, we are truly the "so-so nation."

But we have also seen that religion has become a more important electoral cleavage in recent years, although contrary to claims by some political commentators, so has economics. Moreover, political scientists have written numerous articles and books arguing that national politics is highly polarized, much more so than a generation ago.[1] The national parties are more distinct and more unified.[2] Congress is bitterly partisan. Presidents who received less than 50 percent of the popular vote nevertheless attempt to govern from the left (Clinton in 1993–1994) or right (Bush after 2002) rather than from the center. Once-routine nominations to the federal courts have become occasions for all-out ideological warfare.[3] And the op-ed pages and the political talk shows boil over with partisan and ideological vitriol. Moreover, contemporary "moral" or "values" issues like abortion and gay and lesbian rights were not even on the agenda a generation ago. Looking at the big picture, American politics indisputably has changed. How can we reconcile the view from the grass roots described in the preceding chapters with so many differing views from the treetops?

The key to understanding these inconsistent currents lies in the growing polarization of the political class—officeholders, candidates, party activists, interest group leaders, and political infotainers. Their rhetoric, strategies, and behavior underlie the reality of national polarization, but it is elite polarization that is largely without foundation in a polarized electorate. Even if they still are centrists, voters can choose only among the candidates who appear on the ballot and vote only on the basis of the issues that are debated. Elites nominate candidates and set the agenda, and voters respond.[4] The belief that a culture war rages in the United

---

1 See the essays in Jon Bond and Richard Fleisher, eds., *Polarized Politics: Congress and the President in a Partisan Era* (Washington, DC: CQ Press, 2000).
2 Gary Jacobson, *The Politics of Congressional Elections*, 6th ed. (New York: Longman, 2004): ch. 8.
3 Jennifer Dlouhy, "Senate Traditions a Casualty in Judicial Nominees Spat," *CQ Weekly*, July 12, 2003: 1735–37.
4 On occasion a popular concern makes its way upward and elites are forced to respond. The tax revolt of the late 1970s is an example. Still, it is normally the case that one set of elites responds (the Republicans in the case of the tax revolt), forcing their opponents to do so as well. Note that both parties found it in their interest to downplay budget deficits during the late 1980s. Ross Perot's efforts forced the issue higher on the agenda.

States reflects observations of discourse and behavior within the political class. There, something that might be called a culture war does exist. And since the media are part of the political class and talk mostly to and about the political class, the myth of popular polarization took root and grew.

CENTRIST VOTERS
AND POLARIZING ELITES

For as long as we have had data political scientists have known that political elites are more polarized than the mass of ordinary Americans. That much is only natural—people who take the time and effort to participate in politics or hold office typically have strong feelings about issues. But in the past, electoral pressures constrained how much elites could indulge their own relatively more extreme preferences. In the 1950s, for example, a classic study reported that Democratic National Convention delegates were more liberal than Democratic party identifiers in the electorate and Republican National Convention delegates were more conservative than Republican identifiers in the electorate.[5] But the Republican delegates were further from their rank and file than the Democratic delegates were from theirs. Indeed, on a number of issues, the Democratic delegates were closer to the Republican identifiers than the Republican delegates were! This noteworthy disparity was widely interpreted as a good part of the explanation for the Republican Party's minority status at mid-century. Given the political preferences of the era, only a candidate like Eisenhower—more

---

[5] Herbert McCloskey, Paul Hoffman, and Rosemary O'Hara, "Issue Conflict and Consensus Among Party Leaders and Followers," *American Political Science Review* 54 (1960): 406–27.

moderate than the Republican activists who attended the conventions—could defeat a Democrat. In the old order when the parties followed their hearts rather than their heads, electoral disaster resulted—the Republicans in 1964 when American voters much preferred the echo to the choice,[6] and the Democrats eight years later when voters resoundingly demonstrated their willingness to whack either party when it strayed outside the mainstream.

Much has changed in the past half century, however. We will discuss these changes at greater length in the final chapter, but to sum up their cumulative impact, today's party activists and contributors are less likely to be motivated by material rewards than previously—tens of thousands of public employees no longer worry about losing their jobs if their party loses an election, and legal and programmatic changes have reduced the discretion of public officials to reward the individuals and groups who support them and punish those who oppose them. Moreover, a media ever alert for the scent of scandal watches carefully for material transgressions. Partly as a result of these developments, the old-time party machines with their associated corruption have largely disappeared.

The old-time materially-oriented party organizations for the most part have been replaced by new-style organizations rooted in the advocacy groups that exploded in number after 1960.[7] Intensely concerned with issues, these organizations enroll members (or more often check-writers) who share their ideological and issue commitments. These groups and associations help provide

---

6 One of the Republican campaign slogans was "A Choice, Not an Echo."
7 Kay Schlozman and John Tierney, *Organized Interests and American Democracy* (New York: Harper and Row, 1986); Jack Walker, *Mobilizing Interest Groups in America* (Ann Arbor, MI: University of Michigan Press, 1991).

the money and workers for today's campaigns and in all probability are generating more of the candidacies themselves. The
result is political activists and candidates whose ideological commitments run deeper than a generation ago, whose fear of losing
elections is less than a generation ago, or both. For example, political observers estimate that almost three dozen of the fifty state-
level Republican organizations are under the effective control of
the religious right. In Chapter 4 we noted the polarization of party
activists and strong partisans relative to the lower level of polarization among weak identifiers and independents in the electorate.
Most observers believe that the polarization of the party bases and
elected officials are intertwined.[8]

So long as only one party moves away from the center—like the
Republicans in 1964 and the Democrats in 1972—electoral punishment results, and even ideologically motivated party activists
eventually get the message, as did Democrat activists in the 1980s
who got tired of losing and finally nominated a born-again southern governor who prayed at every opportunity, talked about the
virtues of work and personal responsibility, allowed the execution
of a mentally retarded prisoner to take place, and not incidentally,
won the presidency. But if both parties move away from the center
and locate at a more or less equal distance from the mainstream,
then electoral punishment need not result. Voters will be less
enthusiastic about their choices and about election outcomes than
previously, but given a choice between two extremes, they can only
elect an extremist.

---

[8] For example, Jacobson, *Politics of Congressional Elections*, 248–54; Richard Fleisher and Jon Bond,
"Evidence of Increasing Polarization Among Ordinary Citizens," in Jeffrey Cohen, Richard Fleisher, and
Paul Kantor, eds., *American Political Parties: Decline or Resurgence?* (Washington, DC: CQ Press, 2001).

Before proceeding, we emphasize once again that we are by no means the first to argue that the culture war is an elite phenomenon.[9] But some further development using standard political science theoretical tools enables us to show more precisely how elites can make electoral politics look polarized even when voters are not.

VOTER RESPONSE TO ELITE POLARIZATION

Political scientists often analyze elections with the aid of spatial models. The spatial metaphor is a staple of popular political commentary: candidates run to the right, move to the center, outflank a competitor on their left, and so forth. Spatial models are formalizations of this common metaphor. The simplest model has candidates and voters arrayed along a single dimension, as illustrated in Figure 9.1. The dimension often is interpreted as left-right in the traditional economic sense—level of income redistribution, degree of government control of the economy, and other economic interpretations of economic liberal-conservative ideology. But a dimension can represent any type of issue—more or less strict gun controls, more or less restrictive abortion laws, and so forth. Voters are distributed across the dimension with each one located at his or her "ideal point," a position where their happiness with government policy would be at a maximum. Voters are assumed to like a position less the greater its distance from them.

---

9 See a number of the essays in Rhys Williams, ed., *Cultural Wars in American Politics* (New York: Aldine de Gruyter, 1997). Also E. J. Dionne Jr., *Why Americans Hate Politics* (New York: Simon & Schuster, 1991).

FIGURE 9.1
The One-Dimensional Spatial Model

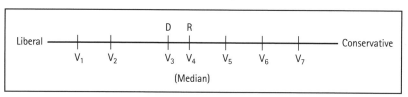

Elections are decided by the positions of the candidates; in a two-candidate contest the candidate closer to a majority of voters wins.

Thus, in Figure 9.1 a Republican who locates at the median of the voter distribution (v_4) will defeat a Democrat who locates to his left at v_3 because the former will get the votes of the median voter (v_4) and everyone to his right (a majority by definition of the median). It can be shown quite formally that with everyone voting, the median is the equilibrium outcome—if two candidates locate at the median, neither can get more votes by moving.[10] This simple model provides the theoretical basis for the (formerly) widely held belief in the centrist tendencies of two-party politics.[11]

To begin our development, consider an idealized version of the 1964 election, as depicted in Figure 9.2. The electorate is normally distributed (that is, bell-shaped) on the economic dimension. Lyndon Johnson is a typical national Democrat who locates somewhat to the left of center (here pictured as one standard deviation from the center) on a dimension representing government intervention in the economy. In contrast, Barry Goldwater is a conservative Republican who wishes to give the voters a choice, not an

[10] Duncan Black, *The Theory of Committees and Elections* (London: Cambridge University Press, 1958).
[11] Anthony Downs, *An Economic Theory of Democracy* (New York: Wiley, 1957).

FIGURE 9.2
Candidate Competition in One Dimension

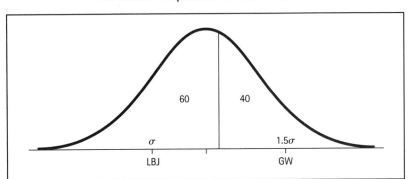

echo. He locates farther away from the center on the right (positioned as 1.5 standard deviations in the figure). The result is that Johnson wins in a landslide with 60 percent of the vote (all those closer to him than to Goldwater, which is about 60 percent with the assumed normal distribution).

But suppose that even when Democrats were winning elections on economic policy there were a second dimension—a moral dimension—that no one noticed because the candidates did not differ on that dimension.[12] That is, voters always have had preferences concerning the moral beliefs and behavior of candidates, but

12 Of course, there could be still other dimensions such as international affairs. We posit two dimensions to keep the exposition simple. The notion that the deep structure of Americans' political attitudes is two dimensional (contrary to Congressional voting) has a long lineage, although the hypothesized content of the second dimension (like the first dimension) varies over time. In 1970 Scammon and Wattenberg warned (correctly) that a class-based Democratic majority was threatened by its dangerous off-center position on the "social issue." In 1984 Maddox and Lillie argued that voters positioned themselves on a personal freedom dimension as well as an economic freedom dimension. In 1995 Shafer and Claggett argued that contemporary politics was organized around two "essentially independent" principles, one economic/welfare and the other cultural/national. And in 2003 Miller and Schofield showed how partisan realignment could occur within a two-dimensional space defined similarly to that of Maddox and Lillie. Richard Scammon and Ben Wattenberg, *The Real Majority* (New York: Coward, McCann & Geoghegan, 1970). William Maddox and Stuart Lillie, *Beyond Liberal and Conservative* (Washington, DC: Cato Institute, 1984). Byron Shafer and William Claggett, *The Two Majorities* (Baltimore: Johns Hopkins University Press, 1995). Gary Miller and Norman Schofield, "Activists and Party Realignment in the United States," *American Political Science Review* 97 (2003): 245–260.

those preferences never came into play forty years ago because candidates projected identical images. All (male) candidates had supportive, loving wives and nice, well-behaved children, professed belief in an Almighty, went to church on Sundays, and in other ways paid homage to the ideal of middle-class morality. Consider that after Nelson Rockefeller divorced in 1962 many Republicans felt that he was no longer a viable candidate. When he remarried a divorcee (with children no less!) in 1963 the pre- and post-remarriage Gallup polls showed a 22 percent swing against him among Republicans.[13] The range of acceptable personal behavior was much narrower at mid-century. Moreover, even if politicians then were secretly more "progressive" on the moral dimension, the media did not expose their transgressions, as revisionist accounts of the Kennedy presidency clearly show. The media at mid-century adhered to a different set of journalistic norms and a different concept of what was newsworthy, a concept that did not include adultery, affairs, drinking, drugs, groping, homosexuality, and other departures from conventional morality.

If voters have preferences concerning both the candidates' economic policies and their moral character and values, we need a two-dimensional representation, as depicted in Figure 9.3. The dynamics of this situation are best illustrated by passing a series of parallel planes through the distribution and focusing on the contours they generate, as in Figure 9.4. Analogous to a topographical map, these contours show the relative distance of voters from the candidates.[14] If we connect the Democrat and Republican positions with a line, the perpendicular bisector of that line separates

---

[13] John Kessel, *The Goldwater Coalition* (New York: Bobbs-Merrill, 1968): 44–45.
[14] For convenience we assume that voters weight the two dimensions equally, which implies that voters prefer the candidate who is closer to them.

FIGURE 9.3
Candidate Competition in Two Dimensions

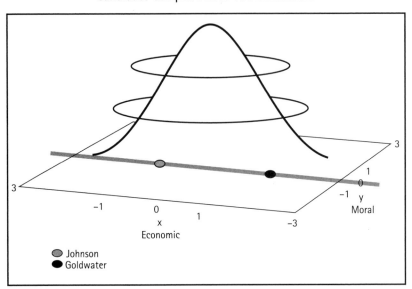

○ Johnson
● Goldwater

the space into voters who are closer to the Democrat (west of the line) and voters who are closer to the Republican (east of the line).

Now assume that while the voters remain in the exact same position in the space, the candidates separate on the moral dimension—Republicans move upward in a more "orthodox" direction and Democrats downward in a more "progressive" direction, with the Democratic candidate closer to the center of the electorate on the economic dimension, and the Republican candidate closer on the moral dimension.[15] We have drawn Figure 9.5 so that the Republican edge on the moral dimension exactly offsets

---

[15] That is, during the Clinton years, public opinion generally favored the Democrat on economic issues but strongly disapproved of Clinton's personal behavior. While Clinton is no longer so prominent on the national scene, the association of the Democrats with unconventional moral views remains.

FIGURE 9.4
Candidate Competition in Two Dimensions: Aerial View

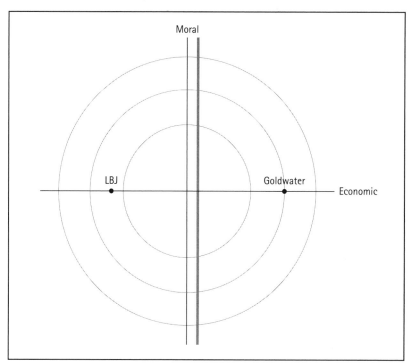

the Democratic edge on the economic dimension—the two candidates are equidistant from the center, but one is closer on economics and the other on morality. In this case the election ends in a tie, roughly what happened in 2000.

Now compare Figures 9.4 and 9.5. By assumption, the voters have not changed: they hold exactly the same positions on the two dimensions and they follow the same behavioral rule—vote for the closer of the two candidates. But notice that the relationship between voters' economic positions and their votes changes

FIGURE 9.5
Democrats and Republicans Separate on the Moral Dimension

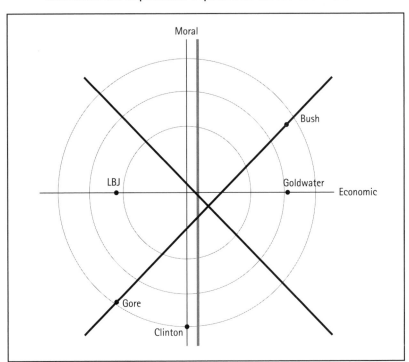

between the figures. The cutting line that separates Republican from Democratic voters rotates to a northwest-southeast orientation: the candidates' electoral coalitions become more heterogeneous on the economic dimension. Bush now gets some support in the northwest from voters who are on the left of the economic dimension, while Gore now gets some support in the southeast from voters who are on the right of the economic dimension—some working class prudes are voting Republican while some Wall Street libertines are voting Democratic. Observing such voters, a casual observer might naturally conclude that economics matters less to voters in Figure 9.5 than in Figure 9.4. And observing that some variable, say, religious commitment, correlates with position on the moral dimension, a casual observer might further conclude that religion now matters more to voters.

These are the wrong conclusions, however justified they seem. By assumption voter positions have not changed, nor has their behavior: each voter supports the candidate closer to his or her (unchanged) position. The observed change in the candidates' support simply reflects the fact that the candidates have separated on the moral dimension. To make this point a little more rigorously, we have carried out a series of computer simulations, as outlined in Figure 9.6. In each simulation voter positions are the same,[16] and the voter decision rule is the same: vote for the closer of the two candidates. But in three steps we change the candidates' positions from those depicted in Figure 9.4 to those depicted in Figure 9.5: the two candidates gradually move apart on the moral dimension until their positions exactly offset their respective positions on the economic dimension. At each of the four stages we carry out a standard political science statistical analysis that relates the voter's presidential choice to his or her positions on the economic and moral dimensions. Figure 9.7 plots the estimated coefficients.[17]

Any analyst looking at Figure 9.7 would view it as persuasive evidence that over the course of the four election series the determinants of the presidential vote have changed significantly: economic position has weakened and moral position has strengthened to the point that both are of equal importance. In a sense,

---

[16] Each simulation uses an identical bivariate normal distribution of voters.

[17] These are logit estimates for the equation Vote = a_1 + b_1 (voter economic position) + b_2 (voter moral position). Coefficients are negative because the farther the candidate is from the voter's position, the less likely the voter is to support that candidate.

FIGURE 9.6
Simulation: Unchanging Voters, Moving Candidates

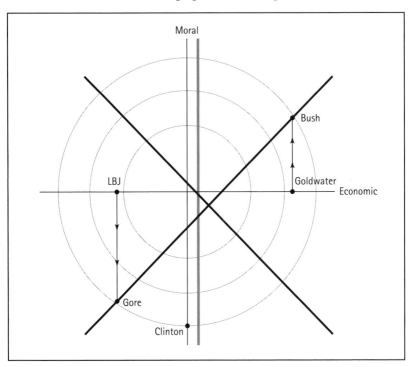

this is true: the correlates of the vote have changed. But this is not because voters have polarized on the moral dimension, nor that they have increased the weight they attach to that dimension (or decreased the weight they attach to the economic dimension)—by assumption voters have not changed. Rather, unmeasured changes in the positions of the candidates make it appear that voters have changed. The point has extremely important (and damaging) implications for literally hundreds of electoral analyses carried out over the past forty years. Because candidate positions generally

FIGURE 9.7
Unchanging Voters Appear to Change As Candidates Move

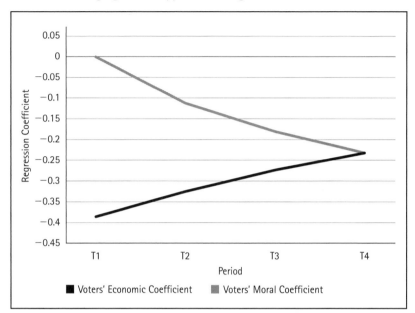

are not measured (how does Dwight Eisenhower compare to Robert Dole? Adlai Stevenson to Bill Clinton?), even when studies use identical measures of voter attitudes, statistical estimates will confound voter change with candidate change.[18]

To return to the real world, we can now put discussions of the culture war in perspective. When candidates diverge (converge) on an issue dimension, voters will appear to weight that dimension more (less) heavily even if their own preferences and decision rules do not change. Thus, when the Republicans nominated libertarian

---

[18] See the Appendix to this chapter for a more detailed explanation.

conservatives like Barry Goldwater and Ronald Reagan and the Democrats nominated economic liberals like Lyndon Johnson and Walter Mondale, all of whom stayed pretty close to the center on the moral dimension, we did not hear much about culture wars.[19] But the Republicans moved closer to the religious right, and then Bill Clinton arrived on the scene. With Bill Clinton the electorate got an admitted adulterer, a confessed marijuana smoker (but not inhaler), and a champion of gay rights. These were pretty clear signals that he was located on the "progressive" side of the moral dimension.[20] Rather than a sudden increase in the political importance of religion to voters, the dramatic rise in the relationship between religiosity and the vote depicted in Figure 7.3 may largely reflect the emergence of Bill Clinton in presidential politics. The 1972 foreshadowing of the stronger relationship is consistent with this hypothesis: the McGovern campaign was associated with what was then called the "counterculture" with its purported rampant drug use and its rejection of traditional sexual mores.

Note that the preceding discussion undermines not only any conclusions about the changing relationship between religiosity and vote, but also analogous conclusions about relationships between religiosity and party identification. Simply substitute Democratic and Republican Parties for Democratic and Republican candidates, and the same conclusion holds. Thus, the common observation that religiosity now is more closely related to party

---

[19] Recall that activists in the religious right complained that Reagan only paid lip service to their issues.
[20] Additionally, Clinton moved the Democratic Party closer to the center on economic issues. Kaufmann is one of the few analysts who have recognized the consequence of such candidate movements when she argues, "As much as any other factor, I believe that the right turn of the Democratic Party on fiscal issues is responsible for the notable salience of cultural issues in the 1990s." Karen Kaufmann, "Culture Wars, Secular Realignment and the Gender Gap in Party Identification," *Political Behavior* 24 (2002): 283–307.

identification may reflect a repositioning of the parties rather than a change in voter attitudes. The Republican Party has become closely allied with white evangelicals, while the Democratic Party has become more assertively secular. Any attempt to compare the correlations between voter positions and political evaluations over time runs the risk of attributing changes in the correlations to changes in voter attitudes when it may be that the positions of the objects of political evaluation—candidates, parties, and groups—have changed.[21]

Before concluding this discussion we emphasize a number of caveats to our discussion. First, we are not claiming as a matter of fact that voters have not changed at all since the 1960s. A generation has passed from the scene and another has been born, not to mention that continuing members of the electorate change their minds as they age and undergo different life experiences. But our argument does show that it is difficult in practice to separate voter change from candidate and party change, and that it is all too easy to mistake the latter for the former. We suspect that such mistakes explain the existence of myths like the culture war. Elites have polarized, but the public opinion data reviewed in Chapters 3–6 provide little reason to believe that elites are following voters. Rather, they are imposing their own agendas on the electorate.

Second, we are not asserting that voter perceptions necessarily are accurate. Aggrieved Democrats may protest our characterizations of President Clinton as a violator of conventional morality

---

[21] For example, Gallup reports that religiosity has become more closely associated with liberal-conservative self-identification. However, if liberal and conservative once were largely economic in their meaning but now have taken on moral or cultural issue connotations, then the argument in the text applies to this claim as well. Frank Newport, "Church Attendance and Party Identification," Gallup News Release, May 24, 2005.

and George W. Bush as an upholder of conventional morality, citing Bush's past alcohol abuse and (unsubstantiated) rumors of cocaine use and extramarital affairs. The reality is not at issue, however; voter perceptions are. And on that score, our depictions are accurate. Despite Clinton's generally high job approval ratings, his personal ratings were always significantly lower and dropped further during his scandal-ridden administration.[22] And a new item on the 2000 National Election Study survey asked respondents whether, since 1992, the country's moral climate had gotten better, worse, or stayed the same. Only 5 percent said it had gotten better, and 45 percent said it had gotten worse.

All in all, it may well be that the myth of a culture war, misconceptions about voter polarization, and mistaken claims about the declining importance of economics all have their roots in the arrival of Bill Clinton on the national scene. The obvious counterfactual would be to observe the voting behavior of the American electorate if the Democrats were to nominate candidates who strongly uphold traditional morality (in actuality, not just in rhetoric).[23] In that event the implication of this analysis would be that the relationship between voter religiosity and candidate choice would be muted.

---

[22] "As the Scandals Have Persisted, Clinton's Standing on Matters of Integrity Has Plunged," *The Public Perspective*, October/November 1998: 24–35.

[23] Senator Joseph Lieberman probably would be the closest example.

APPENDIX TO CHAPTER 9

A Deep Identification Problem in Electoral Studies[24]

During the course of this research we came to the realization that the findings of scores if not hundreds of electoral studies are ambiguous. The problem most deeply afflicts attempts to study electoral change by conducting successive cross-sectional analyses and comparing the results.[25] Typically researchers assume that so long as survey measures are temporally comparable, statistical estimates based on the survey data will be comparable as well. As the examples in this chapter show, however, that is not generally the case.

Consider that in the short span of eight years the popular vote for president in the latter half of the twentieth century varies from more than 60 percent Democratic (1964) to more than 60 percent Republican (1972). How can this variation be explained? The standard way to proceed is to identify a set of predictive variables that are available for all the elections to be analyzed. Such variables would include voters' partisan self-classifications, their ideological self-locations, their ratings of the candidates, and their positions on various issues such as taxation, abortion, racial policies, defense policies, and others.

Often researchers distinguish between "distributional" change and "behavioral" change. The former refers to variation in the distribution of voter attitudes—from election to election there are

---

[24] We thank Michael Herron of Northwestern University for this title.
[25] Rather than point the finger at any of our guilty colleagues, we note an example of the error in Morris Fiorina, "The Electorate in the Voting Booth," in Michael Nelson, ed., *The Parties Respond* (Boulder, CO: Westview Press, 1990): Table 6.4.

fewer liberals, more Democrats, fewer opponents of racial policies, more opponents of abortion policies, and so on. Variations in the number of people who fall into various categories normally will produce electoral change, even if there is no change in the importance people attach to issues or in the relevance of ideological and partisan classifications for voting.[26] Conversely, even if the number of people who fall into various categories does not change, electoral change might still occur because the relative importance of the issues and classifications changes. The latter, represented by different coefficients in statistical models, sometimes is referred to as behavioral change.

But there is a third kind of change that goes unrecognized in cross-sectional studies—changes between elections in the positions of the candidates. Changes in candidate positions are brought into the analysis as qualitative side information that provides a plausible account for any behavioral changes that are uncovered. For example, a number of scholars concluded that voters became more ideological and issue-oriented in the 1960s than in the 1950s (distributional and behavioral changes) in part because of the greater issue and ideological differences in the 1964 and 1968 campaigns.[27] The point we made in this chapter is more subtle than the argument that candidates can affect how voters behave. Our point is simply that candidate change can produce the *appearance* of voter change even in the absence of the latter.

It is relatively easy to determine if average voter positions are constant from election to election, so long as comparable mea-

---

[26] To be precise, this will be the case if the relative probabilities of voting for Democratic and Republican candidates differ among categories that gain and lose people and do not net out in the aggregate.
[27] See the symposium in the June 1972 *American Political Science Review*.

sures of the independent variables are available from election to election.[28] And changes in the distribution of independent variables generally will not result in changes in the coefficients. Thus, distributional change can typically be identified and its effects parsed out.[29] The more serious problem is that in the absence of distributional change, temporal changes in the coefficients can reflect either behavioral change on the part of voters, as discussed above, or changes in the positions of the candidates—as shown in this chapter. If candidates converge (diverge) on an issue it will appear to have less (more) importance to voters even if voters have constant judgments of how important the issue is. Thus, a finding that race has declined as a correlate of voting may mean either that voters judge race to be a less important issue, or that the candidates are taking positions close to each other, or both.[30]

This confounding of effects is not limited to issue variables that explicitly mention distance. Consider the classic party identification scale. Various scholars have attempted to analyze variation in the importance of partisanship across elections.[31] But none of their analyses incorporate the partisanship of the candidates.

---

[28] There is always the question of whether a survey item asked in the context of one election means the same thing when asked in the context of an election thirty years later, but survey researchers rarely discuss that question. A classic example is the apparent change in meaning of the NES "power of the government" survey item. See Norman Nie, Sidney Verba, and John Petrocik, *The Changing American Voter* (Cambridge, MA: Harvard University Press, 1976): 125–28.

[29] Donald Stokes, "Some Dynamic Elements of Contests for the Presidency," *American Political Science Review* 60 (1966): 19–28.

[30] Donald Kinder has pointed out to us that Benjamin Page and Richard Brody showed an intuitive appreciation of this point in an article published a generation ago. They reported that in the 1968 election voter positions on the war in Vietnam had only a weak relationship to presidential vote. Their explanation for this surprising finding was that voters perceived Nixon's and Humphrey's positions as so similar that they ignored Vietnam and decided on the basis of other issues. See Page and Brody, "Policy Voting and the Electoral Process: The Vietnam War Issue," *American Political Science Review* 66 (1972): 979–95.

[31] E.g., Warren Miller, "Party Identification, Realignment, and Party Voting: Back to Basics," *American Political Science Review* 85 (1991): 557–68. Larry Bartels, "Partisanship and Voting Behavior, 1952–1996." *American Journal of Political Science* 44 (2000): 35–50.

That might seem a peculiar statement, given that in each election a Republican opposes a Democrat, but if both parties were to nominate moderate partisans (like a Dwight Eisenhower), one would expect party identification to be less predictive than if both were to nominate hard-core partisans (like a Bob Dole). If one nominates a moderate partisan and the other a hard-core partisan, still other variations in coefficients will result.

The same is true for ideological self-classification. If both parties nominated middle-of-the-road candidates, one would expect ideological self-categorization to matter less, other things being equal, than if a hard-left Democrat ran against a hard-right Republican. Numerous variables that on their face do not seem to be distance variables, on reflection have a distance component that is unmeasured in typical analyses.

So-called proximity measures do not solve the problem because changes in voter proximity to candidates from election to election can reflect changes in voter position, candidate position, or both. Our preliminary simulations indicate that the coefficients on proximity measures vary with changes in candidate positions even when voter positions and voter decision rules stay constant. For example, a finding that relative closeness to the candidate on economic policy matters more than previously may indicate either that voters regard economic policy as more important or that the candidates have moved relatively farther apart, or both.

CHAPTER 10

How Did It Come to This and Where Do We Go from Here?

As its name suggests, political science is a discipline that encompasses both the political and the scientific. In the preceding chapters we have made every effort to practice the "science" part of the compound name—the chapters examine a number of factual claims about contemporary American politics, evaluate their accuracy, offer alternative interpretations of the data, and generally attempt to improve on existing descriptions of the state of our politics. This chapter falls somewhat more under the "political" part of political science. The arguments are broad, the evidence is unsystematic or impressionistic, and the discussion reflects the personal values and judgments of the author. For that reason I absolve my two able associates, Samuel Abrams and Jeremy Pope, from any responsibility for this chapter. Their careful work contributed greatly to any merit the preceding chapters have, but they are not implicated in this chapter, which reflects the views of someone who has been studying, teaching, and writing about American politics for more than thirty years, someone whose affection for the subject has been diminished by its current condition.

Much has changed in American politics since the middle of the twentieth century. Looking back, the interaction of three major developments now seems to me to be of great importance for the state of politics today.[1]

THE ASCENDANCE OF THE PURISTS

In 1962 James Q. Wilson published *The Amateur Democrat*, discussing the rise of the "amateurs" (a term he was not altogether satisfied with), and contrasting them with the "professionals" who had dominated American politics at least since the rise of mass parties in the 1830s.[2] A few years later, Aaron Wildavsky wrote about the "purists" who snatched the Republican Party away from the professionals in 1964 and nominated Barry Goldwater.[3] According to Wilson, the professional

> . . . *is preoccupied with the outcome of politics in terms of winning or losing. Politics, to him, consists of concrete questions and specific persons who must be dealt with in a manner*

---

[1] The discussion that follows draws on and extends the discussion in two of my earlier articles, "Extreme Voices: A Dark Side of Civic Engagement," in Theda Skocpol and Morris Fiorina, eds., *Civic Engagement in American Democracy* (Washington, DC: Brookings, 1999): 395–425; "Parties, Participation, and Representation in America: Old Theories Face New Realities," in Ira Katznelson and Helen Milner, eds., *Political Science: The State of the Discipline* (New York: Norton, 2002): 511–41.
[2] James Q. Wilson, *The Amateur Democrat* (Chicago: University of Chicago Press, 1962).
[3] Aaron Wildavsky, "The Goldwater Phenomenon: Purists, Politicians and the Two-Party System," *Review of Politics* 27 (1965): 386–413.

that will "keep everybody happy" and thus minimize the possibility of defeat at the next election. . . . he sees . . . the good of society as the by-product of efforts that are aimed, not at producing the good society, but at gaining power and place for one's self and one's party.[4]

Wildavsky's characterization of the professional is similar:

The belief in compromise and bargaining; the sense that public policy is made in small steps rather than big leaps; the concern with conciliating the opposition and broadening public appeal; and the willingness to bend a little to capture public support . . .[5]

In contrast, Wilson's amateur

. . . is one who finds politics intrinsically interesting because it expresses a conception of the public interest. The amateur politician sees the political world more in terms of ideas and principles than in terms of persons. Politics is the determination of public policy, and public policy ought to be set deliberately rather than as the accidental by-product of a struggle for personal and party advantage.[6]

Similarly, the distinguishing characteristics of Wildavsky's "purists" are

. . . their emphasis on internal criteria for decision, on what they believe "deep down inside"; their rejection of compromise; their lack of orientation toward winning; their stress on

---

4 Wilson, *The Amateur Democrat*: 4.
5 Wildavsky, "The Goldwater Phenomenon": 396.
6 Wilson, *The Amateur Democrat*: 3.

the style and purity of decision—integrity, consistency, adherence to internal norms.[7]

In these writings a generation ago Wilson and Wildavsky identified the wave of the future. In contrast to the 1950s, we no longer think of the Democrats as a cadre of political professionals leading a broad coalition of blue-collar working people, and Republicans as an opposing cadre leading a smaller but still broad coalition of white-collar professionals and managers. True, unions, especially the public employee unions, continue to play an important role in the Democratic Party, as business does in the Republican, but today we are more likely to think of the Democrats as the party of the environmental, civil rights, pro-choice, gay-lesbian, and gun control groups, and the Republicans as the party of the pro-life, traditional values, antitax and pro-gun groups. Issue activists—Wildavsky's purists—largely define the party images today.

Why the change? To some extent it reflects the decline of material incentives for political participation. The implications of electoral victory or defeat for keeping your job greatly diminished as civil service protection and public sector unionization spread. Similarly, conflict of interest laws, government in the sunshine laws, ethics codes, and investigative media made it harder to reward one's friends and punish one's enemies than a generation ago. As material incentives declined, fewer political activists were drawn from the ranks of people having a personal material stake in political participation.[8] More and more the field was left to

---

[7] Wildavsky, "The Goldwater Phenomenon": 399.

[8] I emphasize the importance of the modifier "personal." Obviously the material consequences of government action are larger today than ever before. But whether you personally benefit from or suffer those consequences today has less to do with your political involvement than in the past. For example, in few cities today would a neighborhood lose its garbage collection for voting the "wrong way."

those with policy or ideological motivations. To the former, compromise was a necessary means to achieving their (material) goals; to the latter, compromise directly devalues their (ideological and programmatic) goals.

The increased importance of money in modern campaigns also contributed to the ascendence of the purists. Understandably, poor people don't contribute.[9] In order to raise money the Democrats had to move upscale and cultivate middle-class issue activists who had money to give. Thus, the economic liberalism of the 1950s Democrats evolved into the lifestyle liberalism of the 1980s. For the Republicans money was in less short supply than voters, so the Republicans allied with conservative Christian groups as a way of attacking the Democrats' majority status. The strategy succeeded, but by the 1990s the activist tail had come to wag the party dog. Thus, the economic conservatism of the 1950s Republicans evolved into the social conservatism that dismayed Barry Goldwater before his death.

Finally, the media has made its contribution to the rise of the purists. People with deep issue commitments who express them in loud chants and strident rhetoric provide good footage and copy. The smallest demonstration will attract a camera crew and give a spokesperson or two the opportunity to provide a colorful quotation or sound bite. Seeing the success of fellow purists in getting recognition by the media, others no doubt were encouraged to follow a similar path. In a 1995 study Jeffrey Barry analyzed all evening news programs on the three major networks plus CNN, and reported that citizens' groups, composed largely of what we

---

9 Sidney Verba, Kay Schlozman, and Henry Brady, *Voice and Equality* (Cambridge, MA: Harvard, 1995): 361–66.

call purists, received a disproportionate share of coverage: "Although they were but a small part of the lobbying population, citizen groups constituted 45.6 percent of all the interviews with interest group representatives, mentions of specific lobbying organizations, and references to interest group sectors."[10]

THE EXPANSION OF GOVERNMENT

A second major development of the past half century is the expansion of government into spheres of life previously considered to be private. In the 1950s the idea that an apartment manager or bank loan officer should not be permitted to discriminate against members of a racial or ethnic minority was a highly contested notion. The idea that a developer could not fill in a swamp because of the presence of a salamander would have seemed ludicrous, let alone the notion that a citizen could petition government for a smoke-free environment.

The literature associates the expanded scope of government with a broad confluence of factors. An increasingly enlightened population demanded that long-festering racial injustices be redressed. An increasingly affluent population turned its attention to quality-of-life issues like the environment. What Mary Anne Glendon called the "rights revolution" enabled citizens to petition the courts for broad remedies to correct newly defined injustices.[11] Whereas rights battles once revolved around such weighty matters

---

[10] Jeffrey Berry, "The Rise of Citizen Groups," in Theda Skocpol and Morris Fiorina, eds., *Civic Engagement in American Democracy* (Washington, DC: Brookings, 1999): 381.
[11] Mary Anne Glendon, *Rights Talk: The Impoverishment of Political Discourse* (New York: Free Press, 1991).

as voting, housing, and employment, aggrieved citizens now assert rights to exercise their dogs in public spaces, to be free of cigarette smoke out of doors, and to breast-feed in public.[12] Once a feminist rallying cry, "the personal is the political" spread far beyond its original context to become a general call for consistency between one's private behavior and public principles. But that consistency could be achieved not only by changing one's private behavior, but also by demanding that the public sector enforce one's personal principles.

Thus, education, affluence, and ideology supported demands for a vast increase in the sphere in which government could operate. The net result of these and other developments was a huge expansion in the jurisdiction of the public sector—the "new social regulation" of the 1960s and 1970s.[13] On the local level Nancy Burns reports a near-tripling in the number of "special districts" (local jurisdictions that deal with environmental, conservation, recreation, and other specific subjects) between mid-century and 1987, from a bit more than ten thousand to about thirty thousand.[14] No one can count the expansion of government as measured in total number of restrictions, regulations, and permits, or in the different areas of life in which government began to operate.

The expansion of the scope of government created myriad new opportunities for those with particular issue concerns to become active in politics. There have always been people who felt

---

12 I am not opposed to such demands; indeed, I am in favor of many of them, but elevating them to the level of rights exaggerates their importance as well as diminishes the importance of fundamental rights.
13 William Lilly and James Miller, "The New Social Regulation," *Public Interest* 47 (1977): 49–62; David Vogel, "The 'New' Social Regulation in Historical and Comparative Perspective," in Thomas McGraw, ed., *Regulation in Perspective* (Cambridge, MA: Harvard University Press, 1981): 155–64.
14 Nancy Burns, *The Formation of American Local Governments: Private Values in Public Institutions* (New York: Oxford University Press, 1994): 6.

extraordinarily strongly about the height and color of neighbors' fences, the contents of children's textbooks, the serving of foie gras in restaurants, and so on, but in past times they were called cranks or busybodies and were generally ignored or left to settle their conflicts informally. Today they are called activists and they demand government action to enforce their views. A party that adopts the narrow agendas of such activists can enlist their energy and resources in support of its candidates.

THE RISE OF PARTICIPATORY DEMOCRACY

At about the same time that ideological and issue motivations for political participation were on the rise, and the scope of government was expanding, the United States experienced a significant participatory turn. Consider Table 10.1, which lists some of the important changes in politics between the elections of John Kennedy and Bill Clinton.

The most widely recognized of these changes is the transformation of the presidential nominating process. In 1960 John Kennedy was nominated by Democratic Party professionals— cigar-chomping "bosses" who met in smoke-filled rooms, according to the popular image. Only four years later Goldwater was nominated by Wildavsky's purists, and eight years after that, opposing purists captured the Democratic party and nominated George McGovern, taking advantage of new rules changes that established the contemporary primary and caucus process.[15]

---

[15] Theodore White, *The Making of the President 1972* (New York: Bantam, 1973), especially Chapter 2.

TABLE 10.1

Changes in American Politics Since 1960

Presidential nominating process

"Candidate-centered" politics

Open meetings

Recorded votes

Expanded rules of standing

Enhanced judicial review

Open bureaucracy

Intervenors

"Maximum feasible participation"

Proliferation of local bodies

Advocacy explosion

Propositions

Proliferation of polls

New technologies

This transformation of the nomination process was only the most visible step in a move away from party-centered elections toward candidate-centered elections.[16] Soon political scientists noticed that a significant incumbency advantage had developed in elections for the House of Representatives: Incumbents could win comfortable victories by emphasizing their personal characteristics, constituency service, and individual records even in areas

---

[16] Martin Wattenberg, *The Decline of American Political Parties, 1952–1996* (Cambridge, MA: Harvard University Press, 1998).

seemingly more hospitable to the opposing party.[17] For their part voters seemed to be putting less weight on their party affiliations, and party cohesion in government broke down as individual officeholders sought to win the support of an increasingly volatile electorate.[18]

Government in the sunshine gained in popularity. Legislatures, boards, and councils around the country opened up their proceedings, allowing citizens to attend and to speak to a greater extent than previously considered advisable in a representative democracy. These same government bodies opened their heretofore closed deliberative proceedings to the public as well. And, increasingly, the actions of elected officials entered into the public record, as legislatures abandoned voice, standing, and other forms of anonymous voting in favor of recorded votes.

Both the courts themselves and Congress liberalized rules of standing so that citizens could use the courts to a much greater extent than previously.[19] A nature lover who had not suffered personal material damage from a new dam could not sue on behalf of salmon in 1960. Today such a right is taken for granted.[20] In associated developments courts that at one time had largely deferred to administrative rule-makers began to take an increasingly active and aggressive role in overseeing the administrative process.[21] Congress even subsidized intervenors in bureaucratic proceedings

---

[17] Gary Jacobson, *The Politics of Congressional Elections* (New York: Longman, 2001): 125–32.

[18] For a recent survey of these developments see Morris Fiorina, "Parties and Partisanship: A 40-Year Retrospective," *Political Behavior* 24 (2002): 93–115.

[19] Richard Stewart, "The Reformation of American Administrative Law," *Harvard Law Review* 88 (1975): 1169–1813.

[20] As a member of Trout Unlimited I certainly regard this as an advance in social welfare.

[21] R. Shep Melnick, *Regulation and the Courts* (Washington, DC: Brookings, 1983).

and allowed them to collect legal fees for challenging agency actions in the courts.

At the local level "maximum feasible participation" became the watchword of the time as the federal government used its sticks and carrots to open up local politics to new groups and subsidized the formation of such groups. And as we noted earlier, there was a huge increase in local government jurisdictions of various types.[22]

Meanwhile an advocacy explosion occurred as thousands of new groups organized and engaged in political activity.[23] Sometimes they circumvented uncooperative legislatures by sponsoring propositions—the use of propositions surged between 1960 and 2000.[24] Politicians became increasingly aware of popular reaction to their actions as polling became a pervasive feature of contemporary society, and new technologies that at first enabled politicians to better advertise to constituents soon got turned around as citizens' groups realized they could use the same technologies to pressure politicians.

In short, these changes and others stripped away the insulation that had long surrounded political institutions and processes, leaving them more exposed to popular scrutiny and far more open to popular participation. Seemingly American democracy became more democratic. Or did it?

---

[22] According to the U.S. Census Bureau, there are now about 86,000 governmental jurisdictions in the United States, most of them at the local level.

[23] Kay Schlozman and John Tierney, *Organized Interests and American Democracy* (New York: Harper and Row, 1986); Jack Walker, *Mobilizing Interest Groups in America* (Ann Arbor, MI: University of Michigan Press,1991); Jonathan Rauch, *Government's End: Why Washington Stopped Working* (New York: Public Affairs, 1999).

[24] A trend decried by some of our leading political commentators. See David Broder, *Democracy Derailed: Initiative Campaigns and the Power of Money* (New York: Harcourt Brace, 2000).

THE HIJACKING OF AMERICAN DEMOCRACY

The three developments just discussed (along with others I have no doubt overlooked) have cumulated and interacted to produce the present disturbing state of American politics. How they have is not immediately obvious. For although government bodies make laws and issue regulations applying to a vastly larger range of economic and social activities, there are also vastly increased opportunities for Americans to participate in making those laws and applying those regulations. The problem is that relatively few people take advantage of those opportunities. Mostly, the purists do.

For most Americans, attending lengthy meetings of city councils, school boards, or planning commissions is not something high on the list of favorite ways to spend an evening. Relaxing after a hard and stressful day's work, spending a little time with the kids, or enjoying a few hours of recreation generally come first. Similarly, when it comes to ways to spend a Saturday afternoon, attending a caucus comes in well below almost anything other than a dentist appointment. Whatever the literal meaning of the Greek, Aristotle is best translated as "Man is by nature a social animal," because the more common alternative "Man is by nature a political animal" is clearly wrong. Most people do not take inherent pleasure in political activity. For most of us, it is costly in time, energy, and resources that we would prefer to devote to other activities. Almost half of us do not even bother to vote in presidential elections. As the young Robert Putnam wrote,

Most men are not political animals. The world of public affairs is not their world. It is alien to them—possibly benevo-

lent, more probably threatening, but nearly always alien. Most men are not interested in politics. Most do not participate in politics.[25]

Who does participate? Who takes advantage of the multitudinous new opportunities to attend evening meetings, write checks, and work in campaigns? While there are a variety of reasons people participate, ranging from the social to the material, probably the most general is that the people who participate are for the most part those who care intensely about some issue or some complex of issues. They have deep policy, programmatic, or ideological commitments. That seems completely obvious—people who care expend their time, energy, and other resources to participate. People who do not care do not make the effort. One does not need a Ph.D. to point that out.

The problem is that people who care deeply also tend to have extreme views on the issues they care deeply about, as we noted in Chapter 2. The first observations to this effect were made by social scientists three-quarters of a century ago, and no doubt politicians have understood the association between intensity and extremity since the first chieftains heard the angry rumblings around the campfires eons ago.[26] Intensity and extremity go together as illustrated by the pairings of common political descriptors. We regularly read and hear about raging liberals but not raging moderates, rabid conservatives but not rabid middle-of-the-roaders, wishy-washy moderates but not wishy-washy liberals or

---

[25] Robert Putnam, *The Beliefs of Politicians* (New Haven, CT: Yale University Press, 1973): 1.
[26] Floyd Allport and D. A. Hartman. "The Measurement and Motivation of Atypical Opinion in a Certain Group," *American Political Science Review* 19 (1925): 735–60. See also Hadley Cantril, "The Intensity of an Attitude," *Journal of Abnormal and Social Psychology* 41 (1946): 129–35.

conservatives, bitter partisans but not bitter independents.[27] To have an intensely held position generally is to hold a relatively extreme position, and vice versa.

Thus, not only is the desire to participate not very widely distributed in the general population, there is a strong bias in how it is distributed. The extremes are overrepresented in the political arena and the center underrepresented. The standard example is the party activists who dominate the presidential selection process. Activists are small minorities even within their own parties—the highest recorded turnout in the Iowa caucuses was 12 percent of the voting age population in 1988 when both parties had competitive nomination contests. Generally the turnout percentage is in single digits. In January of 2004 some 120,000 of the most committed Democrats turned out to vote in the Iowa caucuses, about one-sixth as many as the 740,000 Iowans who voted for John Kerry in November. The situation is similar in the issue battles waged by the various cause groups. As we discussed in Chapter 5 the terms of the abortion debate are set by the 10 percent or so of the population that occupy each tail of the distribution of abortion attitudes, while the three-quarters of the population of "pro-choice buts" goes largely unheard. Extremists march, work in campaigns, give money, and otherwise push their views more strongly than do moderates.

I emphasize that this pattern of biased participation is broad and pervasive. It extends well beyond partisanship and a few

---

[27] In a column about the Middle East, Thomas Friedman calls for more "fanatical moderates." Similarly, John Avlon wants more "fighting centrists, militant moderates, and middle-of-the-road warriors." See Thomas Friedman, "Wanted: Fanatical Moderates," *New York Times Op-ed*, November 16, 2003: 4–13. John Avlon, "Wanted: Fighting Centrists," realclearpolitics.com, May 28, 2005.

prominent issues like abortion, and it extends well below the national level as well. Indeed, the bias may be worst on the local level. Consider the following recent illustration from San Francisco.[28] Residents began complaining that someone was using axes and chain saws to girdle mature trees (eucalyptus, Monterey Pines, and cypress) on city property. Anti-environmentalists? Antisocial vandals? On investigation it turned out that it was citizen tax dollars at work. The city Recreation and Park Department contains a unit called the Natural Areas Program (NAP), which has both paid staff and volunteers. The trees were a casualty of a NAP master plan that among other things called for the eradication of "alien species." On further investigation it turned out that NAP volunteers had already begun restoring poison oak (a native species) to some city parks, and that future plans included replacing the turtles at a city lake with a more genetically correct species of tortoise.

San Francisco is an extremely liberal city and its residents yield to no one in their greenness, but even in San Francisco poison oak does not enjoy majority support. Having been made aware of what one of its tiny specialized agencies was up to, the Park Department appointed an advisory panel to oversee the NAP, "but then it was discovered that most of the organizations on the list [of advisory panel members] consisted of similar native plant supporters."[29] City supervisors then reconstituted the panel to include park users and elected officials.

---

[28] This vignette is drawn from Ken Garcia, "S.F. Residents Battling Plant Lovers—Little-Known Group Chopping Down Trees," *San Francisco Chronicle* April 23, 2002: A-13, and "Poison Oak Activists Restrained," *San Francisco Chronicle*, October 1, 2002: A-13.
[29] "Poison Oak Activists Restrained": A-13.

While this may seem like an extreme example, lesser examples at the local level are legion. A local official working in concert with a small constituency of committed issue activists formulates a proposal or plan that is far out of the mainstream of community sentiment (environmental and land use restrictions probably are the most common, but sex education in the schools provides some wild examples). At some point the proposal makes it onto the radar screens of normal people who do not participate in obscure government proceedings, a dust-up occurs, and the proposal is rejected or the program revised or terminated amidst acrimonious charges by activists and popular disbelief by normally inactive people.

In addition to pushing unrepresentative views on specific issues, two other characteristics of purists are worthy of note. The first is that the issues that motivate them often are different from those that are of most concern to the great mass of ordinary citizens. Most citizens want a secure country, a healthy economy, safe neighborhoods, good schools, affordable health care, and good roads, parks, and other infrastructure. Such issues do get discussed, of course, but a disproportionate amount of attention goes to issues like abortion, gun control, the Pledge of Allegiance, medical marijuana, and other narrow issues that simply do not motivate the great majority of Americans. For example, despite the attention it receives in the political arena, abortion does not even register on lists of what citizens say are the most important issues facing the country.[30]

---

30 Eight polls by five different polling organizations in 2002–2003 asked a version of the "most important problems facing the country" item. None received enough abortion responses to report them as a separate category. www.pollingreport.com/ prioriti.htm, accessed January 5, 2004.

Gun control is another particularly illustrative issue.[31] A large majority of the country favors "common sense" gun control provisions—background checks, trigger locks, higher minimum age requirements, registration, prohibitions of high-capacity clips, and so on. But most Americans do not believe that additional restrictions will do much good. Perhaps for that reason few people feel very intensely about gun control—one national poll in the aftermath of Columbine had gun control twelfth in importance on a list of voting issues. Antigun and pro-gun activists are another story, of course, and they fight tooth and nail over what most Americans view as a relatively minor issue. Al Gore staked out a strong position on the issue in 2000, apparently to appeal to gun control activists in the Democratic primaries.[32] A more moderate position on gun control probably would not have cost him any blue states, but it might have kept enough hunters in the Democratic fold (or out of the electorate) to swing 2 percent of the vote in Ohio or Missouri or Tennessee, or 1 percent in New Hampshire. Had Gore carried even one of these states, he would have won the 2000 election—Florida would have been irrelevant.

Finally, because purists hold their views more intensely than ordinary people do, their operating style differs from that of most people. They are completely certain of their views: they are right and their opponents are wrong. Moreover, their opponents are not just misguided or misinformed, but corrupt, stupid, evil, or all three. There can be no compromise because truth does not

---

[31] The discussion in this paragraph draws on Morris Fiorina and Paul Peterson, *The New American Democracy*, 3rd ed. (New York: Longman, 2003): 150–152.
[32] In addition, Gore's strong antigun position may have been part of his attempt to appeal to women voters on child safety issues.

compromise with error. Their issues are too serious to permit any levity to enter the discussion. Angry attacks substitute for reasoned discussion.[33]

Most adult Americans spend their daily lives working in organizations where courtesy and civility are basic presumptions of how people should interact with each other. Moreover, discussion and negotiation underlie normal decision-making processes in the organizations and institutions of civil society and the economy. Americans contrast the environments in which they live their lives with a political order dominated by activists and elected officials who behave like squabbling children in a crowded sandbox.[34] This is another reason why Americans dislike politics: they are put off by the people who specialize in politics.[35]

In sum, there is a disconnect between the world of contemporary Americans and the political order that purports to represent them. Citizens see a political order that characteristically debates policy proposals more extreme than necessary to address societal issues and community problems, a political order that spends inor-

---

[33] During one radio show that I appeared on, a caller who identified himself as an activist commented that if he were arrested, he didn't want a centrist defense attorney. The comment is revealing of the mindset of the activist. Politics is like a trial in which one side wins and the other loses. Emphasize evidence in favor of your side, no matter how weak. Ignore evidence in favor of the other side, no matter how strong. Winning is the only thing that matters. Hibbing and Theiss-Morse have shown that ordinary Americans have a very different view about how government should work—it should be a cooperative, problem-solving process. While Hibbing and Theiss-Morse regard such an ideal as immature and unrealistic, I am more sympathetic. John Hibbing and Elizabeth Theiss-Morse, *Stealth Democracy* (Cambridge, England: Cambridge University Press, 2002).

[34] The fact that most people now get their news from television probably heightens this impression. In a recent article Mutz and Reeves report that "when viewers are exposed to televised political disagreement, it often violates well-established face-to-face social norms for the polite expression of opposing views. As a result, incivility in public discourse adversely affects trust in government." Diana Mutz and Byron Reeves, "The New Videomalaise: Effects of Televised Incivility on Political Trust," *American Political Science Review* 99 (2005): 1. If these findings generalize, they suggest that normal Americans are more put off by the incivil style of contemporary political discourse than by disagreement itself.

[35] An Arizona state representative told me that he would look around the ballroom at his election night parties and think "these are the only parties these people ever get invited to."

dinate amounts of time debating policy issues that most citizens do not view as among the more important issues facing the country, and a political order dominated by a political class whose behavior and operating style would be unacceptable outside of politics. Citizens hardly can be blamed if they increasingly regard government as something that tries to do things *to* them rather than *for* them, something best kept at a distance. As Matthew Miller comments, "Alienation is the only intelligent response to a political culture that insults our intelligence."[36]

THREE IMPORTANT CAVEATS

By this point some readers may suspect that my vision of American politics is some kind of utopia akin to *Mr. Rogers' Neighborhood*, where all of us are friends. Far from it; I do not think that in the absence of purist domination of democratic political processes we would all spend our days sitting around singing "Kumbaya." Conflict is the human condition, and conflict is the basis of politics—conflict of wants, conflict of interests, and conflict of values. As Madison wrote in Federalist 51, "But what is government itself but the greatest of all reflections on human nature? If men were angels, no government would be necessary." Government is a necessary evil. Evil because it is inherently coercive and its operations restrict the liberty of some citizens.[37] Necessary, because in its absence even greater evils would occur as a result of some exercising their unrestricted liberty. All I mean to

---

36 Matthew Miller, "Is Persuasion Dead?" nytimes.com, June 4, 2005.
37 As George Washington put it, "Government is not reason, it is not eloquence—it is force."

argue in the preceding pages is that the political order that now exists in the United States creates unnecessary conflicts and indulges itself in conflicts that are the concern of relatively small numbers of unrepresentative people. Often this comes at the expense of attention to conflicts that concern larger numbers of citizens and leads to inattention to policy solutions that would be widely viewed as progressive.[38]

A second, even more important, caveat is that the changes in American politics outlined in the preceding pages are by no means all bad. Few would argue that the United States was better off as a society before the mid-1960s expansion in the scope of government. The great progress toward ending racial discrimination alone falsifies any such claim. Similarly, the treatment of women, the handicapped, the aged, and other vulnerable categories indisputably has improved society. So has the treatment of our environment and our natural resources. Like my colleagues who are economists, I believe that in many cases there were more efficient and less coercive ways to achieve many of these laudable goals, but if the choice is between what government did and its having done nothing, the answer seems clear to me. My argument is simply that when combined with the participatory turn, the expansion in the scope of government allowed various kinds of fanatics to exert an undue degree of control over the political agenda.

---

[38] A number of recent books propose bold policy proposals to meet important problems in the area of health care, education, and Social Security, as well as point out that political stalemate keeps such proposals off the agenda. My aim in this book has been to explain why the political order is unable and even unwilling to address problems that concern millions of ordinary Americans in a pragmatic non-ideological manner. See for example, Michael Lind and Ted Halsted, *The Radical Center: The Future of American Politics* (New York: Anchor, 2002); Matthew Miller, *The Two Percent Solution* (New York: Public Affairs, 2003). For a forerunner, see E. J. Dionne Jr., *Why Americans Hate Politics* (New York: Simon & Schuster, 1991).

A final caveat should go without saying, but I have learned from various talks that it does not. Nothing in these pages advocates the suppression of minority points of view. Sometimes extremists are right and a majority eventually adopts their once-extreme views. The abolitionists held views that most at the time considered extreme, and certainly the intensity with which some of them held their views was demonstrated in arenas like Bloody Kansas and events like John Brown's raid. Intense minorities have every right to freedom of speech and association, and when peaceful advocacy proves futile, they can engage in civil disobedience. When they do, they should expect to be sanctioned by the societal majority: over time their sacrifices may convince society of their views. That said, there is no reason to support a political order that disproportionately enhances the power of intense minorities.

CAN ANYTHING BE DONE?

"Clowns to left of me, jokers to the right, here I am, stuck in the middle with you."
(from Stealer's Wheel, *Stuck in the Middle With You*)

The chorus of this 1973 pop hit could well serve as the anthem of normal Americans. How might we diminish the influence of the clowns and jokers and expand the influence of the middle? I am not optimistic. There will be no help from the political class itself. The activists who gave rise to the notion of a culture war, in particular, and a deeply polarized politics, in general, for the most part are sincere. *They* are polarized. Active members of conservative Christian groups allied with the Republican Party sincerely believe they are fighting a culture war, as do active members of pro-choice and gay rights groups allied with the Democratic Party. That they are small, unrepresentative minorities does not alter the fact that these and numerous other interest group activists feel strongly about their issues and will vote, work, and contribute in support of them.

Nor will most politicians be of much help. Like interest group activists, many candidates and officeholders sincerely believe they are engaged in a war. Some are themselves purists who were activists before winning office. Others see instrumental reasons for acting like purists. Each party has a base composed of people particularly sensitive to certain issues. Increasingly, professional campaigners seem to believe that mobilizing the base is the most important component of a winning electoral strategy, a belief that may be a self-fulfilling prophecy if appeals to the base result in moderate voters turning off and tuning out. So, however misplaced from the standpoint of the welfare of the larger country, an emphasis on cultural and other conflicts not of particular interest to the majority appears to be an integral part of contemporary electoral politics.

The media potentially could be of some use. When an activist spokesperson makes a pronouncement, a critical media could ask "How many citizens do you speak for?" "When did they appoint you as their spokesperson?" "Have they approved your message?" The media could even cease its unconsidered use of the neutral term "activist" and use terms that are often more accurate—exhibitionist, crackpot, blowhard. None of this will come to pass however, for despite pious pronouncements about the role of the media as the guardian of democracy, the media consist largely of profit-sector enterprises that will continue to behave as such. That means an emphasis on differences among Americans rather than commonalities. The commercial success of the newspapers and news shows depends on good story lines, and conflict is a good story line. "Americans agree on core values" is not a headline that editors expect to sell newspapers. "Citizens describe themselves as moderates" is not a good lead for the evening news. A red and blue battleground over which the Democrats and Republicans wage war is a news frame that fits the selection principles of the news industry.[39]

Political scientists are notoriously loath to suggest reforms. As a profession we tend to be conservative with a small "c." One reason is that more than most people we realize how little we genuinely know about the operation of complex political processes and institutions, and, consequently, how likely it is that proposed reforms will prove ineffectual or, worse, counterproductive. The long, frustrating history of campaign finance reform is a good example, but arguably, almost all reforms have had some unforeseen negative consequence. Nevertheless, I offer several possibilities that might improve our politics, although I stress that these are not magic bullets, either alone or in combination. Moreover, although they would probably increase the representativeness of electoral politics at the state and national levels, they would do little to redress the unrepresentative nature of local politics that requires time-consuming participation in the deliberations of councils and boards. The latter seems to me to be a more difficult problem.

---

[39] I hope I am wrong. The decision by CNN to terminate *Crossfire* certainly was a positive step.

PRIMARY REFORM

In Chapter 9 we discussed how the abstract median voter model provides the logic underlying the traditional observation that two-party competition has centrist tendencies.[40] In the real world, however, that abstract logic can be overridden by factors not in the model. One of these factors is primary elections that select the candidates who will stand in the general election.

In 1994 California Republican Governor Pete Wilson won reelection in a landslide, Republican candidates won four of the six other statewide races for state office, and Republicans defeated four Democratic House incumbents. Seemingly, Bill Clinton's 1992 victory in the state had been only a hiccup in a long Republican era that began with the election of Ronald Reagan as governor in 1966. That appearance was short-lived. In 1996 Clinton hammered Republican Robert Dole in California, and four years later Al Gore easily bested George W. Bush. The hapless condition of the California Republican Party became strikingly clear in 2002 when they could not defeat Gray Davis, a personally lackluster Democratic governor who had mishandled a state energy crisis and allowed a historic budget crisis to develop. In fact, Democrats won all the statewide races in 2002 for the first time in California history. In less than a decade California had changed its hue from dark red to dark blue.

What happened? The California Republican Party was captured by its extreme social conservative elements, and its electoral

---

[40] When there is more than one issue dimension there is generally no equilibrium, but a variety of alternative solution notions nevertheless continues to support the conclusion of centrist tendencies in two-party competition.

fortunes promptly plummeted.[41] Many analyses identify Senator Barbara Boxer as one of the most liberal members of the U.S. Senate, seemingly a candidate vulnerable to defeat at the hands of a Republican moderate, but she is a two-time winner. Similarly, the unasked question in the 2003 recall of Democratic Governor Davis was how such an unpopular governor, saddled with energy and budget crises, could have been reelected in the first place? The answer both to Senator Boxer's survival and to Davis's reelection lies in the old political saw that "you can't beat somebody with nobody." In primary elections California Republicans nominate hard-core conservatives whose appeal is too limited to defeat even flawed Democratic candidates.[42]

In 1996 almost 60 percent of California voters, including majorities of both registered Republicans and Democrats, approved Proposition 198, a ballot initiative sponsored by Tom Campbell, the kind of Republican social moderate who has trouble winning California primaries.[43] The proposition called for a

---

[41] Although the reversal of Republican and Democratic fortunes in California often is attributed to the growth in the proportion of minority, especially Latino, voters, preliminary analysis indicates that the areas of greatest Republican loss were economically upscale areas that registered relatively high levels of support for environmental and gun control initiatives, and relatively low levels of support for antiabortion and antigay initiatives. Josh Benson, "From Reagan Country to Clinton Capital: The Political Transformation of California," Senior Thesis, Stanford University Political Science Department, 2003.

[42] Boxer was initially elected in 1992, running against Bruce Herschensohn, a far-right Los Angeles radio and TV commentator. In 1998 she handily defeated a Republican who flip-flopped on abortion and gay rights as he was caught between the conservative party base and the larger more moderate electorate. Her luck held in 2004 as she easily defeated an under-funded central valley Republican who never managed to get any electoral traction. In 2002 Davis was narrowly reelected running against Bill Simon, a conservative businessman with little political experience. Interestingly, less than a year after reelecting Davis, a larger number of Californians than had voted in 2002 turned out to recall him, and a larger number than had voted for Davis in 2002 voted to replace him with Arnold Schwarzenegger, a political novice. In the exception that proves the rule, Schwarzenegger is the kind of socially moderate Republican who can win elections in California. The unusual nature of the recall election saved the California Republican Party from itself.

[43] Campbell had lost to Herschensohn for the honor of opposing Boxer in 1992. Many political analysts thought he would have defeated Boxer had he gotten through the primary.

"blanket primary," a novel system in which all voters—Democrats, Republicans, minor party adherents, and the nonaligned—
can work their way down the same ballot, voting for a Democratic candidate for one office, a Republican candidate for
another, a Libertarian candidate for yet another, and so on, with
the leading vote getter in each party for each office advancing to
the general election. The intent was to increase turnout and to
dilute the extreme voices who dominate closed primaries by
allowing moderate candidates to win by attracting the support of
(an increased number of) Independents and moderate members of
the opposing party. Called the "blanket" primary by its supporters, critics derided it as a "free love" primary (because voters
did not have to make any commitment to a party). Both major
parties as well as various minor parties immediately filed suit to
overturn the blanket primary as an unconstitutional infringement
on their rights of free association, such unified opposition by the
parties confirming many voters' beliefs that the blanket primary
was a good idea.[44]

The challenge wended its way through the courts until in 2000
the U.S. Supreme Court by a 7–2 margin held for the parties and
threw out the blanket primary.[45] My sympathies lie with the two
dissenters (Justice Stevens joined by Justice Ginsburg), who did not
understand why the associational rights of political parties should
outweigh the right of voters to structure the electoral process—the

[44] "Part of its appeal may have been its antagonists. State GOP Chairman John Herrington bemoaned
the appeal to 'the mindless middle,'" Ronald D. Elving, "Californians Explore 'Jungle Primaries.'"
1996. *Pundits & Prose*, CNN-All Politics. www.cnn.com/allpolitics/1996/analysis/pundits.prose/
elving/elving1.shtml, accessed November 19, 2003. For wide-ranging discussions of California's experience with the blanket primary see Bruce Cain and Elisabeth Gerber, eds., *Voting at the Political Fault
Line* (Berkeley, CA: University of California Press, 2002).
[45] *California Democratic Party et al v. Jones.*

very basis of democratic government, *whose operation they pay for*—however they please. But Justice Scalia, who wrote for the majority, explicitly noted the constitutionality of other primary formats, such as Louisiana's nonpartisan run-off primary.[46] In this primary, all the candidates for the same office are listed together. If one candidate wins a majority of the vote on the first round, he or she is elected. If not, the top two finishers wage a second, run-off campaign to determine the winner.

The run-off primary should have somewhat the same consequences as the blanket primary. Given more choices one would expect more voters to participate, and moderate Republicans or Democrats might defeat more extreme partisans with the support of independents and moderate voters from the other party. That possibility troubles hard-core partisans of both parties, of course. The worst outcome is to lose an office, but a close second is to win it with a candidate of your own party insufficiently committed to your principles; some hard-core partisans even rank the second outcome lower than the first.[47]

The problem with nonpartisan run-off primaries inheres in one of their many nicknames. Sometimes called "jungle primaries," they allow the distinct possibility that fringe candidates can make the runoff, as when David Duke, a former member of the Ku Klux Klan, made the runoff for governor of Louisiana in 1991. It is highly unlikely, although not impossible, that such candidates can

[46] Ibid., 18.
[47] On the Republican side, the Club for Growth has increasingly mounted primary challenges to insufficiently pure Republicans. After an unsuccessful attempt to defeat incumbent Republican Senator Arlen Specter of Pennsylvania, the Club's leader commented "Obviously, we want to win. But our members always said it's better to lose with Toomey than win with Specter." John Cochran, "GOP Primary in Pennsylvania Sends Mixed Message to Party Leaders," *CQ Weekly*, May 1, 1004: 1018.

win a major state office if they made the runoff against either a Republican or Democrat, but with several Republicans, several Democrats, and various other candidates on the ballot, the top two finishers might have relatively small proportions of the total vote and neither may have very widespread appeal. Still, high thresholds (signatures, filing fees) for making the ballot can reduce the number of fringe candidates, and the desire of voters not to waste their votes on long shots or no shots should work in favor of candidates with broad appeal.

REDISTRICTING REFORM

As we noted in Chapter 2, recent national elections have been exceedingly close—*in the aggregate.* This is most apparent in elections for the House of Representatives since 1996, where the parties have split the aggregate vote nearly evenly and control of the House has been at stake in each election. But despite the close division of the aggregate vote as well as the close division of seats, when we look a bit closer at the statistics, an interesting feature of congressional elections emerges: as elections have gotten closer in the aggregate, the number of competitive elections has declined. In 2000, when the presidential race was a cliff-hanger, only seventy-four of the 435 House seats were won by margins of less than 55 percent. In 2004, another close presidential election, but after the decennial reapportionment and redistricting cycle, the number of such competitive districts fell to 24.

The number of competitive congressional districts declined in the mid-1960s and stayed low through most of the 1970s and

1980s. Although redistricting was suspected as a cause of that earlier decline, academic research found little support for that suspicion.[48] Competition increased in the 1990s but then fell in 2000 and fell again in 2002. Many (not all) observers believe that the redistricting that occurred in 2001–2002 had a good bit to do with this more recent decline in competitive seats—the parties behaved conservatively, concentrating on protecting their seats rather than attempting to capture those of the opposition.[49] The result was a bipartisan gerrymander that left almost 90 percent of U.S. House seats safely in the hands of one or the other of the two parties, despite the close division of the aggregate vote.[50]

To consider the theoretical effect of alternative districting arrangements, consider the simplified example illustrated in Figures 10.1A and 10.1B. A hypothetical state consists of 40 percent Democrats, 40 percent Republicans, and 20 percent Independents. The state is rectangular in shape and people are evenly distributed over its area, but partisans are concentrated: the Democrats all live in the northern two-fifths of the state, Republicans in the southern two-fifths, Independents in the middle fifth. Assume the citizens elect a five-member legislature from single-member districts of equal population. Among the many possibilities, one would be to draw five districts horizontally, as in Figure 10.1A.

---

[48] John Ferejohn, "On the Decline in Competition in Congressional Elections," *American Political Science Review* 71 (1977): 166–76. For a more recent and more conditional analysis cf. Gary Cox and Jonathan Katz, *Elbridge Gerry's Salamander* (Cambridge, England: Cambridge University Press, 2002).
[49] Gregory Gilroux, "Remap's Clear Trend: Incumbent Protection," *CQ Weekly*, November 3, 2001: 2627–32.
[50] Bruce Oppenheimer questions this conventional wisdom, arguing that increasing residential homogeneity is a more important factor. "Deep Red and Blue Congressional Districts: The Causes and Consequences of Declining Party Competitiveness," in *Congress Reconsidered*, Lawrence Dodd and Bruce Oppenheimer, eds. (Washington, DC: CQ Press, 8th ed., 2005): 135–57.

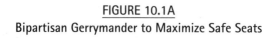

FIGURE 10.1A
Bipartisan Gerrymander to Maximize Safe Seats

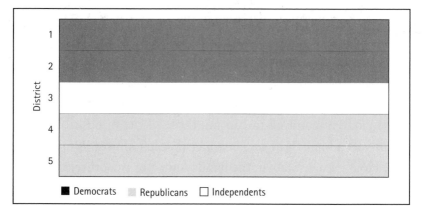

This districting arrangement results in two safe Democratic districts in the north, two safe Republican districts in the south, and one competitive district in the middle.

Alternatively, one could draw district lines vertically, as in Figure 10.1B. This districting arrangement would result in five competitive districts, each containing equal numbers of Democrats and Republicans, with Independents holding the balance.

Politics under the alternative districting arrangements probably would be much different. Under the horizontal arrangement, the safe Democrats and Republicans only fear a primary challenge, since the other party has no support in their areas. In the middle district the Democrat or Republican who did better among Independent vote would be elected, presumably encouraging the contenders to take more moderate positions.

Under the second districting arrangement, all the districts would be competitive. A party could win anywhere from none to

FIGURE 10.1B
Redistricting to Maximize Competitive Seats

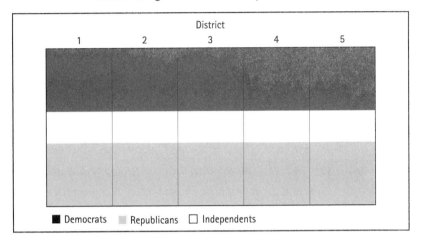

five seats in an election, but no one could win with the support of only their partisans. Independents hold the balance in all districts, providing an incentive for the candidates to appeal to the middle.[51]

In addition to their effects on the positions of candidates within districts, other things being equal, having more competitive districts increases the likelihood that the out-party can win control of the legislative chamber. Thus, the legislature as a whole is more accountable to the electorate as a whole when a large number of competitive seats make party majorities precarious.[52] The prospect

---

[51] Although some early studies discounted the moderating effects of close elections, a comprehensive study of candidate positioning in 1996 supports the existence of an incentive to move toward the center under competitive conditions. See Steven Ansolabehere, James Snyder and Charles Stewart, "Candidate Positioning in U.S. House Elections," *American Journal of Political Science* 45 (2001): 142–45.

[52] Steven Ansolabehere, David Brady and Morris Fiorina, "The Marginals Never Vanished?" *British Journal of Political Science* 22 (1992): 21–38.

of losing their legislative majority likely will make party leaders a little more cautious about pushing extreme policies.[53]

Since the important one-person, one-vote decisions handed down by the U.S. Supreme Court in the mid-1960s, the court has intervened actively in the legislative redistricting process but so far has limited its conception of equal representation. The courts closely examine population equality, demanding a degree of inter-district equality that is truly preposterous.[54] And the courts have willingly taken up challenges involving questions of racial fairness. Until very recently, however, the courts have hesitated to consider the question of partisan or bipartisan gerrymandering.[55] In *Vieth v. Judelirer*, decided in April 2004, a 5–4 majority of the U.S. Supreme Court declined to invalidate a Pennsylvania redistricting plan on the grounds that it was an unconstitutional partisan gerrymander. The court left open (barely) the possibility of considering future cases, however, so the courts may extend their reach in the coming years.

In sum, another avenue toward moderating American politics would be to remove redistricting from the purview of legislatures

---

[53] Thomas Brunell points out that creating homogeneous Republican and Democratic districts maximizes the number of partisans who will be happy with their own representative, and demonstrates empirically that such voters evaluate Congress more positively than those represented by members of the other party. While true, this argument (1) ignores the preferences of Independents (more than one-third of the population), and (2) does not address the more general question of whether a legislature composed entirely of members from safe seats will function as well as one whose members endure greater electoral competition. Thomas Brunell, "Rethinking Redistricting: How Drawing Districts Packed with Partisans Improves Representation and Attitudes Towards Congress," (in press) *Political Science and Politics*

[54] For example, in a 2002 Pennsylvania decision, a three-judge panel of the Federal Appeals Court threw out a redistricting plan because the most and least populous districts differed by nineteen residents. Because of errors, deaths, births, and moves, census data are not accurate to within nineteen residents in a congressional district (approximately 650,000 people) by the time they are recorded, let alone by the time the first election in the new districts occurs. Jonathan Allen, "Court Puts Pa. Primaries in Doubt," *CQ Weekly*, April 13, 2002: 963.

[55] In a partisan gerrymander, one party attempts to screw the other. In a bipartisan gerrymander both parties agree on a plan to divvy up the seats.

and place it in the hands of (preferably nonpartisan) appointed commissions. But rather than have the legislature approve the final plan, skip the legislature and submit it to popular referendum.[56] Still, we caution that such a reform is unlikely to produce major changes. After all, the Senate has polarized as much as the House of Representatives, and redistricting is irrelevant there, suggesting that redistricting is only a minor part of the explanation for congressional polarization, or that it is important only in combination with other factors such as closed primaries.

INCREASING PARTICIPATION

If political participation is correlated with greater intensity and extremity of views, then other things being equal, any increase in participation entails an increase in participation by less intense and less extreme people. Thus, reforms that increase participation have the potential to lower the decibel level of American politics and increase its attentiveness to mainstream concerns. The obvious targets are reform of registration and voting procedures that would make both easier. Political scientists have given this subject a good deal of attention and the most detailed research suggests that maximum easing of registration and voting procedures would increase turnout in presidential elections by 8 to 15 percentage points.[57]

---

[56] In many states this would not be as politically difficult as might first appear. In 2005 California Governor Arnold Schwarzenegger proposed a ballot initiative providing for commission redistricting in California beginning in 2006. Democrats in the legislature offered to adopt such a proposal so long as it did not take effect until after the 2010 census—legislators are term-limited so they would not be affected so long as the implementation date were delayed!

[57] Ruy Teixeira, *The Disappearing American Voter* (Washington, DC: Brookings, 1992): Ch. 4.

In his 1997 presidential address to the American Political Science Association, Arend Lijphart called for compulsory voting, an idea utterly foreign to Americans but widely accepted in other world democracies.[58] Unfavorable comparisons of voting turnout in the United States with turnout elsewhere generally omit any mention that 90+ percent turnout figures in other democracies often are produced by compulsory voting laws. Usually these levy fines for failure to vote, although Greece provides for jail terms, a penalty that is never enforced. Italy uses a mixture of carrots and sticks, subsidizing travel back to one's place of registration, but stamping nonvoters' papers with "did not vote" and posting their names on community bulletin boards. Judging by the outraged reaction of my students, the principal objection to such laws is that people should not be forced to vote when they may not like any of the candidates. This objection could be easily met—permitting submission of a blank ballot, or putting a "none of the above" option on the ballot, for example.

There is a vein of political science research that discounts the political effect of increased turnout. Analysts make the counterfactual assumption that everyone votes, and then compare the distributions of political attitudes and candidate preferences between the hypothetical expanded electorate with those in the actual electorate. Such analyses typically report only small differences.[59] Without plunging deeply into a discussion of false consciousness, the problem with such analyses lies in the assumption that "other things remain the same." If the presidential electorate were to

---

[58] "Unequal Participation: Democracy's Unresolved Dilemma," *American Political Science Review* 91 (1997): 1–14.
[59] Teixeira, *Disappearing American Voter*: 86–101 reports his own results and summarizes others.

nearly double, and the off-year electorate to nearly triple, it is likely that parties and candidates would make different appeals to capture the support of the new voters who would now be showing up at the polls. There is no reason to believe that their preferences would be the same as when they are not in the electorate. In particular, if it were known that a huge influx of politically unattached, relatively moderate people were going to vote, the incentive for candidates to move toward the center would increase.

While I sympathize with Professor Lijphart's argument for compulsory voting, the major problem with advocating it seems to me a practical one. Americans are called on to vote so frequently that it would be unreasonable to require them to vote on any and all occasions when elections were held.[60] Most other democracies vote far less often for far fewer offices than Americans do. The only way compulsory voting would be feasible in the United States would be to "combine up" elections, as was the case roughly between the 1870s and the 1940s. Elect presidents, governors, U.S. Representatives, and state and local officials, as well as vote on propositions, bond issues, and so forth on the same day. Even so, with primaries added in, and shorter terms of office than elsewhere, compulsory voting still would ask a lot of the electorate.

Perhaps we need a concerted effort to think outside the box of traditional forms of participation. These involve physical presence in most cases, and that is too high a price to pay for many or most contemporary Americans, especially at the local level.[61] But we

---

60 Anthony King, *Running Scared: Why America's Politicians Campaign Too Much and Govern Too Little* (New York: Free Press, 1996).
61 I have the greatest respect for the motives of theoretically minded colleagues who advocate strong forms of deliberative democracy, but as an empirically minded social scientist I think their proposals run counter to everything we know about mass political behavior.

are in the midst of a revolution in communications technology that might open up entirely new avenues of political participation. Much nonsense has been written about electronic town halls, instantaneous referenda voting, and so forth, but we should not throw out the baby with the bathwater. It may be that the often-decried ability of splinter groups to locate each other over the Internet is more than offset by the far greater ease of mass participation that the Internet allows. To note the most obvious possibility, at some future date, when Internet connections are as ubiquitous as telephones, it might be possible to require that before taking effect every board or council decision must receive the electronic votes of a majority of a given percentage of the citizenry in its jurisdiction.[62] Any such proposal would need thorough public debate, of course, but it illustrates the kinds of new democratic possibilities that may be available to our children.[63]

THE NUCLEAR OPTION:
ANOTHER PARTY?

In May of 2005 the political class was transfixed by a fight to the death in the U.S. Senate over the filibustering of presidential appointments to the federal courts. Republican Majority Leader Bill Frist, frustrated with obstructionist Democratic tactics, and reportedly eager to gain the support of social conservatives for a 2008 presidential run, was about to exercise the "nuclear option"

---

[62] In the New England town where I once lived, concern that low attendance at Town Meeting was producing unrepresentative decisions stimulated some residents to advocate a requirement that any Town Meeting decision should appear on the ballot at the next regularly scheduled town election before taking effect. Betsy Bilodeau, "It's Time to Change Town Meeting," *Concord Journal,* March 5, 1998: 7.
[63] The debate already has begun. See, for example, Jennifer Stromer-Galley, "Voting and the Public Sphere: Conversations on Internet Voting," *PS: Political Science and Politics* 36 (2003): 727–31.

(so named by former Republican Majority Leader, Trent Lott), using a parliamentary maneuver to allow a simple majority to end the filibustering of presidential appointments. Senate Democrats viewed this plan much as Roman Senators viewed Caesar crossing the Rubicon and promised to plunge the Senate into civil war.

As the two sides prepared to engage, members of the political class were startled by polls reporting that a majority of the American public was paying little attention to this celebrity death match.[64] Some members of the Washington press corps were aghast—each day might bring Armageddon and the public was not engaged?![65] They should not have been surprised. Not only was the public paying little attention to the whole affair, but a significant plurality thought that both parties were acting like spoiled children instead of devoting their energies to solving real problems.

The filibuster fight was the political class at its worst. Republicans and Democrats had drawn lines in the sand that could not be crossed, and both parties danced to the tune played by their group allies who had decreed that any compromise was unthinkable. After Armageddon was averted by a bipartisan deal of the kind that used to be common, bitterly disappointed activists assailed the "Gang of 14"and the traitorous Republican "cabal." The public, in contrast, viewed the deal as a rare eruption of common sense in Washington.[66] Outside of the political class, few Americans

---

[64] "Confirming Judges, *CBS News Poll*, released May 23, 2005. David Moore, "Public Conflicted in Filibuster Debate," *Gallup Poll Release*, acccessed May 24, 2005.
[65] Phone calls to author from Washington journalists.
[66] I do not mean to discount the importance of the filibuster fight. The outcome had important political consequences and the controversy raised serious questions about constitutional government. Having watched both Democratic- and Republican-appointed federal judges usurp the power of legislatures for thirty years I have long favored subjecting all federal judges to electoral approval (as most of our states do), or limiting their terms to 8–10 years, or requiring extraordinary majorities to confirm them. Rather than a filibuster I would prefer a constitutional amendment to do the latter.

define independent judgment as marching in lockstep behind party leaders or genuflecting before extreme cause groups.

Recognizing the increasingly obvious disconnect between the contemporary political class and normal Americans, some of our national commentators have begun to float the possibility of a third-party or extra-party movement. After noting the organizational and fund-raising possibilities of the Internet, *Los Angeles Times* columnist Ronald Brownstein muses:

> . . . *if the two parties continue on their current trajectories, the backdrop for the 2008 election could be massive federal budget deficits, gridlock on problems like controlling health-care costs, furious fights over ethics and poisonous clashes over social issues and Supreme Court appointments. A lackluster economy that's squeezing the middle-class seems a reasonable possibility too.*
>
> *In such an environment, imagine the options available to Sen. John McCain (R-Ariz.) if he doesn't win the 2008 Republican nomination, and former Sen. Bob Kerrey of Nebraska. . . . If the two Vietnam veterans joined for an all-maverick independent ticket, they might inspire a gold rush of online support—and make the two national parties the latest example of the Internet's ability to threaten seemingly impregnable institutions.*[67]

In a similar vein, *New York Times* columnist David Brooks warns

> *There's going to be another Ross Perot, and this time he's going to be younger. There's going to be a millionaire rising*

---

[67] "Internet, Polarized Politics Create an Opening for a Third Party," www.latimes.com, April 25, 2005.

out of the country somewhere and he (or she) is going to lead a movement of people who are worried about federal deficits, who are offended by the horrendous burden seniors are placing on the young and who are disgusted by a legislative process that sometimes suggests that the government has lost all capacity for self-control.[68]

And noting the rapid increase in registration of Independents in states that register by party, John Avlon speculates

. . . if the two parties insist on rejecting independent voters by nominating polarizing conservative and liberal candidates, 2008 could be the year that a strong centrist independent is elected president as part of a bipartisan national unity ticket.[69]

The obstacles to a successful third party movement in the United States are daunting, of course. Not since the 1850s when the Republicans replaced the crumbling Whigs has one of the two major parties been replaced. Among many institutional obstacles, nearly all states use a winner-take-all system to allocate their electoral college votes.[70] So, while Ross Perot received almost 19 percent of the national popular vote in 1992, he won no electoral votes.

Still, parties can be transformed. The New Deal Democrats were not the same party as the southern-dominated party that won only two of the nine presidential elections held between 1896 and 1928. Nor was the Republican Party under Ronald Reagan

---

[68] "In the Midst of Budget Decadence, a Leader Will Arise," *New York Times*, February 19, 2005, Section A, page 15.

[69] John Avlon, "2008: The year a strong centrist independent becomes President?" www .radicalmiddle.com/x_avlong_2008.htm.

[70] This is not a constitutional provision, of course. Thus, part of a successful third party movement might include requiring states to allocate electoral votes in proportion to their popular votes.

the same as the party that won only two of the nine presidential elections held between 1932 and 1964.

One type of reason parties change is "exogenous" in social science jargon—coming from outside the system. Prime examples include sociological changes that fracture old coalitions and provide building blocks for new ones, as suburbanization and the growth of the Sunbelt helped weaken the New Deal coalition and remake the modern Republican one.[71] Other reasons are "endogeneous," coming from within the system. An example is new leaders who search for new electoral strategies after a string of electoral losses has weakened old leaders and delegitimized their strategies, as Democrats like Bill Clinton did in the late 1980s. The two kinds of change are not mutually exclusive. How politicians react to exogenous change can make or destroy majorities, arguably the latter in the case of the New Deal Democrats and their reaction to the movement of African Americans from rural south to urban north.[72]

Some Democrats today pin their hopes on exogenous sociological changes,[73] but there is nothing inevitable about these—it takes human volition to channel them in political directions, and it is difficult to appreciate them until after the fact. For now that leaves endogenous possibilities. It is not likely that change will come from the Republican side. After all, they are winning. But change on the Democratic side is no more likely—although the Democrats are losing, they are not losing badly, as they did in the

---

[71] Nelson Polsby, *How Congress Evolves: Social Bases of Institutional Change* (New York: Oxford University Press, 2004).
[72] Thomas Edsall with Mary Edsall, *Chain Reaction* (New York: Norton, 1992).
[73] John Judis and Ruy Teixeira, *The Emerging Democratic Majority* (New York: Scribner, 2002).

1980s. Indeed, one wing of the party continues to argue strenuously for even purer adherence to the strategies that have made them a minority.

This suggests that only an insurgent movement large enough to cost one party the election could provide sufficient motivation to remake the party by co-opting the insurgents. An insurgency on the left flank (e.g., Nader) or right flank (e.g., Buchanan) is not the answer—any additional votes captured on the flank likely would be more than offset by votes lost in the center. Rather, as Brownstein, Brooks, and Avlon suggest, a successful insurgency would come from the center. (Perot's supporters lay "between" Republicans and Democrats.[74])

Certainly there is plenty of opportunity. Many Americans today see their electoral choice as between a Republican Party that dreams of dismantling the federal safety net and a Democratic Party that sees tax increases as the only tool for reforming it. Between a Republican Party that has abandoned fiscal responsibility for "borrow-and-spend" and a Democratic Party that has never credibly renounced its historic commitment to "tax and spend." Between a Republican Party that equates crony capitalism with free enterprise and a Democratic Party in thrall to public sector unions with vested interests in preserving the status quo and raising government spending. Between a Republican Party whose appointees subjugate empirical evidence to religion and ideology and a Democratic Party whose activists hold mainstream religion

---

[74] "When asked to locate their own positions on the issue scales, Perot voters consistently fell in between the Clinton and Bush voters. . . . Perot tended to fare best among voters who scored toward the middle on the balance of issues measure . . . ." Paul Abramson, John Aldrich, and David Rohde, *Change and Continuity in the 1992 Elections* (Washington, DC: CQ Press, 1994): 192–93.

and values in contempt. And between a Republican Party whose neoconservative ideologues advocate foreign policies they fear are recklessly antagonistic and a Democratic Party whose Michael Moore wing they suspect does not truly believe that the United States is the best country that ever existed.

Personally, I hope Avlon, Brooks, and Brownstein are prescient.

Index